Toward a Homiletical Theology of Promise

Toward a Homiletical Theology of Promise

The Promise of Homiletical Theology

Volume 4

Edited by
DAVID SCHNASA JACOBSEN

CASCADE *Books* · Eugene, Oregon

TOWARD A HOMILETICAL THEOLOGY OF PROMISE

The Promise of Homiletical Theology 4

Copyright © 2018 Wipf and Stock Publishers. All rights reserved. Except for brief quotations in critical publications or reviews, no part of this book may be reproduced in any manner without prior written permission from the publisher. Write: Permissions, Wipf and Stock Publishers, 199 W. 8th Ave., Suite 3, Eugene, OR 97401.

Cascade Books
An Imprint of Wipf and Stock Publishers
199 W. 8th Ave., Suite 3
Eugene, OR 97401

www.wipfandstock.com

PAPERBACK ISBN: 978-1-5326-1391-3
HARDCOVER ISBN: 978-1-5326-1393-7
EBOOK ISBN: 978-1-5326-1392-0

Cataloguing-in-Publication data:

Names: Jacobsen, David Schnasa, editor.

Title: Toward a homiletical theology of promise / David Schnasa Jacobsen, editor.

Description: Eugene, OR: Cascade Books, 2018 | Series: The Promise of Homiletical Theology | Includes bibliographical references.

Identifiers: ISBN 978-1-5326-1391-3 (paperback) | ISBN 978-1-5326-1393-7 (hardcover) | ISBN 978-1-5326-1392-0 (ebook)

Subjects: LCSH: Preaching. | Bible—Homiletical Use.

Classification: BV4222 .H9 2018 (paperback) | BV4222 (ebook)

Manufactured in the U.S.A.   04/13/18

New Revised Standard Version Bible, copyright 1989, Division of Christian Education of the National Council of the Churches of Christ in the United States of America. Used by permission. All rights reserved.

Contents

Contributors | vii
Acknowledgments | ix

Introduction | 1
—*David Schnasa Jacobsen*

1 The Promised Land: A Postcolonial Homiletic of Promise in the Asian American Context | 9
—*Sunggu Yang*

2 A Promising, Trivocal Hermeneutic for Twenty-First-Century Preaching: Justice, Transformation, and Hope | 28
—*Kenyatta R. Gilbert*

3 The Spirit-Breathed Body: Divine Presence and Eschatological Promise in Preaching | 51
—*Ruthanna B. Hooke*

4 A Homiletical Theology of Promise: More Than One Genre? | 69
—*Paul Scott Wilson*

5 Promissory Kerygmatics | 87
—*James F. Kay*

6 Promise as an Event of the Gospel in Context: Toward an Unfinished Homiletical Theology of Grace and Justice | 106
—*David Schnasa Jacobsen*

Bibliography | 121

Contributors

Kenyatta R. Gilbert, Associate Professor of Homiletics, Howard University School of Divinity

Ruthanna B. Hooke, Associate Dean of Chapel and Associate Professor of Homiletics, Virginia Theological Seminary

David Schnasa Jacobsen Professor of the Practice of Homiletics and Director of the Homiletical Theology Project, Boston University School of Theology

James F. Kay Joe R. Engle Professor of Homiletics and Liturgics and Dean and Vice President of Academic Affairs, Princeton Theological Seminary

Paul Scott Wilson, Professor of Homiletics, Emmanuel College, University of Toronto

Sunggu Yang, Assistant Professor of Christian Ministries, George Fox University

Acknowledgments

With this final volume in the series, The Promise of Homiletical Theology, I want to begin by thanking the people of Cascade Books. My editor, Rodney Clapp, has been particularly helpful along the way. I am grateful for his patience, his assistance with questions, and conversations together over coffee and breakfast at AAR/SBL these last few years. James Stock, Matthew Wimer, and Brian Palmer have also been of great help—both with this and other volumes. I am grateful for Cascade's faith in the promise of this series from first to last.

I cannot forget to thank my PhD students at BUSTH, especially Revs. Duse Lee and Yohan Go, who have helped with this and other books in the series. They have been more than just research assistants, but have served as helpful consultants on important decisions along the way. Revs. Go and Lee are, in fact, homiletical theologians in their own right. I am already looking forward to their contributions to the field. They both have a theological depth and a commitment to the church that inspires me deeply.

I wish also to express my thanks to Dean Mary Elizabeth Moore. She has supported and encouraged my research in the Homiletical Theology Project from the beginning. I am fortunate to be a part of the vibrant research culture that is Boston University School of Theology. Dean Moore's support has made that a living reality and, for me, a time of scholarly renewal as well.

Finally, I wish to thank my Vanderbilt University doctoral mentor and friend, David G. Buttrick, who died just before this volume was completed in late April, 2017. It was David Buttrick who from first to last kept pushing me to think of preaching as a truly theological activity. He challenged me as an MDiv student at Vanderbilt in the mid 1980s when he was teaching and writing books like his landmark *Homiletic: Moves and Structures* (1987) and *Preaching Jesus Christ: An Exercise in Homiletic Theology* (1988). When I returned to Vanderbilt in the 1990s to work on a PhD in homiletics with the same Professor Buttrick, I again enjoyed his doctoral seminars. David Buttrick continued to argue strongly for a turn to theology with his own published work in *A Captive Voice: The Liberation of Preaching* (1994) and in turn his lifetime of scholarship, thanks to the guidance of editors Tom Long and Edward Farley, generated a wonderful *Festschrift* whose title says it all, *Preaching as a Theological Task: World, Gospel, Scripture* (1996). I frankly just could not get enough of Buttrick's intellectual breadth, his lover's quarrel with the church, his curmudgeonly cantankerousness, and above all his unfailing grace and love for justice. True to form, David Buttrick saw to it that his funeral at Benton Chapel at Vanderbilt was not so much about him, but a witness to the resurrection of Jesus Christ. I, from first to last, have been inspired by him and thus hope that these words, these four volumes of very human words about homiletical theology, point away from themselves to the Mystery David himself brooded about and longed to name into the world again. Even though it would likely make you wince, I thank you, David Gardner Buttrick. *Soli deo Gloria.*

>Season of Easter, 2017
>David Schnasa Jacobsen
>Boston, MA

Introduction

—David Schnasa Jacobsen

Promise has long been a way of characterizing gospel theologically. It has also not been the province of any one theological tradition, either. Promise shows up a with a difference already in Galatians and Hebrews, it is an object of theological reflection among Donatists like Tyconius and in their famous opponent, Augustine of Hippo. You can find significant references to it in theologians as distinct as Luther, Calvin, and Wesley. Today, promise is big among confessional theologians like Jürgen Moltmann and deconstructive radical theologian John Caputo. There is something about promise that compels traditions to think and rethink themselves in relation to gospel. There is also something elusive about promise that compels any cultural tradition to keep working through the gospel mystery to which it points.

That is precisely the attraction of promise for what I keep calling the "unfinished task" of homiletical theology. Theology done within "earshot" of hearers both anchors in promise as a basic predisposition to a God of grace and justice and holds promise back to God in contexts and situations of injustice and profound suffering. For me, promise is powerful because it understands gospel as something ever being "given" and yet groaning for its realization. It is not a homiletical theology of the gospel that comes in neat packaging, it is both the "correlative of faith" in hearing, as contributor James Kay notes, and the locus of profound struggle among hearers in all their difference. For preachers called to announce promise it is a gift and an ongoing, unfinished theological task.

This final volume in the series *The Promise of Homiletical Theology* seeks to focus on different ways promise can be understood and named in preaching. The presupposition in most of these pages is that promise offers a core sense of what the gospel is in relation to context. That said, this relationship entails a profound cultural sensibility. Promise does not sound the same in a white, mainline parish as it does in an African American congregation or a Korean immigrant church. A core sense of promise finds a quite different reception in relation to contexts. This is why the language of "core sense" or "character" of promise are the words we use here to discuss how it functions as gospel. It is not a fixed, universal content; it does not sound the same or taste the same in every time and place. This idea is in keeping with Edward Farley's vision of gospel not as some preserved essence, but an emerging "opening" named anew in every time and place:

> [Gospel is] not a thing to be defined. It is not a doctrine, a delimited objective content. The summaries in Acts and in Paul of what is proclaimed, the formulas of the kerygma, attest to this. Phrases like the kingdom of God, Jesus as Lord, Christ crucified do have content, but that content is not simply a quantity of information. To proclaim means to bring to bear a certain past event on the present in such a way as to open the future. Since the present is always specific and situational, the way that the past, the event of Christ, is brought to bear so as to elicit hope will never be captured in some timeless phrase, some ideality of language. Preaching the good tidings is a new task whenever and wherever it takes place.[1]

Promise is like that. It is not a thing, but an action, an event *in context* that, as speech act theorists remind us, also has an illocutionary force: it *does* something. It is at the same time something perplexing. It may awaken faith and hope, but it is also just as likely to awaken profound dissatisfaction with the status quo and unjust orderings of reality. For this reason, it cannot be simply one more formula, one more catch phrase, and certainly no one-size-fits-all gospel solution for cultural traditions. If anything, the dissonance in promise is what calls forth dialogue between those traditions—a dialogue that will not likely leave those traditions the same.

And so we contributors to this volume gather in these pages to gesture "toward a homiletical theology of promise" in our very different contexts. This particular set of chapters is born from a consultation at the Academy of Homiletics Annual Meeting in San Antonio, Texas, in November, 2016. The six participants were invited to write papers focusing on the following research question:

> "The language of promise is key for a theology of grace that runs from Paul through Augustine to Luther and into twentieth-century neo-Orthodox theology. At the same time, language around

---

1. Farley, *Practicing Gospel*, 80.

promise has also shaped the eschatological hopes for justice and reconciliation in liberation and political theologies (e.g., Moltmann). Homileticians as different as James Kay, Eunjoo Mary Kim, David Lose, Dawn Ottoni Wilhelm, Kenyatta Gilbert, Paul Scott Wilson, Sally Brown, Christine Smith, and David Schnasa Jacobsen relate promise in various ways to their theological reflections on matters like the gospel, the authority of scripture, the task of narration, commitments to justice, and prophetic preaching. How might a homiletical theology of promise aid our struggle with the relationship of God's justice and grace in context? Papers focusing on a contextual theology of the gospel in relation to promise, and also the place of eschatology with respect to a homiletical theology of grace and justice are especially welcome. Contributors may also wish to draw on a variety of theories to help articulate the importance of promise for their homiletical theologies: especially speech-act theory, narrative theory, and philosophical and theological hermeneutics."[2]

Given the diversity of ways a homiletical theology of promise can be formed, we move toward a key point of struggle. How is it that homiletical theologies of promise ground both claims of divine presence in grace and divine commitment to justice? The goal here is to see different homileticians, from different theological positions and cultural traditions wrestling with a theology of the gospel in context that takes promise seriously.

Behind this, of course, is some emerging sense of just what homiletical theology is. As this four-part series of books has unfolded, homiletical theology has been understood and practiced across several different intersections. Historically, homileticians do their theological work in five crucial areas, many of which they hold in common with other kinds of theologians: theologies of the gospel, theologies of preaching, theologies of Word and Sacrament, theology in the content of preaching, and preaching as a kind of theological method. While this is true especially for scholarship in homiletical theology, that is, among the guild of those who teach and do research in homiletics, there is another sense that homiletical theology is not theirs alone, but belongs more deeply to the practice of preaching itself. Charles Bartow has argued that homiletical (theological) criticism takes three forms: scholarly, professional, and pedagogical.[3] The scholarly form, we've just discussed. The professional form inheres in the practice of preaching itself: preachers are,

---

2. This research question was adapted from #5 on my web site for the Homiletical Theology Project, http://www.bu.edu/homiletical-theology-project/research-questions/ (accessed March 1, 2017).

3. Bartow, "Homiletical (Theological) Criticism," 154–57.

in essence, front-line theologians for whom homiletical theology necessarily happens in the Sunday to Sunday task of preaching. It is in their professional vocation of being reflective practitioners where a theological habitus or disposition is formed. The practice of preaching is not just where theology is franchised from the systematicians. Instead, the sermon is where theology is done rhetorically and fostered conversationally, through language that is at once theological but also imagistic, metaphorical, and narrated. Pedagogical homiletical theology, finally, is the kind of theological formation that happens in the homiletics classroom and in situations of mentorship. Here preaching is first surfaced not just as a technical enterprise, but a theological one that touches at the core of one's life as wisdom/habitus at an existential-personal level—which is to say, again with Edward Farley, that we preachers may not all be systematic theologians, but we are all, even students in preaching class, theologians in this dispositional sense.[4] These crucial distinctions become especially important in this volume. Our various takes on "promise" are not only different contextually, but vary in terms of the homiletical-theological intersection explored, and in one case, considers homiletical-theology beyond its purely scholarly form. On the one hand, this makes the work as a whole more troubling to delineate—just what is homiletical theology anyway? On the other hand, the fact that homiletical theology does its work in different ways and at different levels also reflects its ongoing vitality. This volume toward a homiletical theology of promise in relation to context invites readers to consider the homiletical-theological task in all of its complexity and richness.

That being said, it is also good to reflect back on the history of promise sketched in the first few pages of this book. Promise sounds different when Paul, an apostle, is trying to help the Galatians respond to Christian Judaizers than it sounds to the writer of Hebrews, for whom promise is an invocation of the great exemplars of faith and the great cloud of witnesses who preceded them.[5] Promise also functions differently for Tyconius, a bit of an outlier among Donatists, and Augustine who invokes promise in *On Christian Doctrine* quite possibly to push back against Donatist understandings of scripture, teaching, and church. Despite the fact that Luther, Calvin, and Wesley place promise at the center of their theological work in justification, they do not sound the same at all when matters shift to sanctification, Christian vocation, or the possibility of "social holiness." For that matter, even contemporary

---

4. Farley, *Theologia*, 35–36.

5. Craig Koester carefully points out the subtle differences between Paul's treatment of promise, covenant, and law and Hebrews' treatment of the same in *Hebrews*, 110–15, esp. p. 115. For the connection of promise to Christ and faith in Paul and Hebrews, see Attridge, *The Epistle to the Hebrews*, 313–14.

theologians end up using promise for different purposes—to push back on a Christian theology that has forgotten its eschatological moorings in Moltmann and to resist any confessional theology in the form of a Derridean non-foundationalist radical theology in Caputo. As much as promise has occupied the tradition, and impacted ways it has thought about the theological task of preaching and the way it names gospel in context, it has never really been homogenous at all. Contemporary homileticians who receive promise as gift and presence, are animated by promise in seeking justice, and struggle with promise in the face of injustice and suffering are in good company.

That is what we have convened here: a group of homiletical theologians for whom promise means different things in context and for whom promise poses unique struggles in the practice of preaching.

This is demonstrated most clearly as we anticipate the chapters to come. Each author brings a unique set of questions around promise and anticipates its different contextual embodiments across a variety of homiletical-theological intersections.

In chapter 1, Sunggu Yang places the language of promise squarely in the context of the Asian American immigrant experience. His contribution, "The Promised Land: A Postcolonial Homiletic of Promise in the Asian American Context," weaves together deep contextual reflection and a profound intercultural understanding of promise that is especially poignant for Asian American immigrants who must negotiate a three-fold identity that is Asian, American, and Christian. The language of promise for Yang has more than Biblical valence, it also has intercultural power when brought into relation with the promise of the American Dream and the profound difficulty of immigrant life in a racialized land. This, in fact, becomes a central metaphor for Yang's analysis: it is the various understandings of promised land in Asian culture, American culture, and Christian identity that becomes central for his work in reconfiguring the language of promise in a postcolonial mode—which opens up the possibility of an engaged, transformative vision for the pilgrim Asian American church.

Kenyatta Gilbert offers a powerful contribution toward a homiletical theology of promise with his "A Promising, Trivocal Hermeneutic for Twenty-First-Century Preaching: Justice, Transformation, and Hope." Using his own striking research into the tri-vocal hermeneutic of prophet, priest and sage in connection to the African-American preaching tradition, Gilbert asks the question: "How might the use of the scriptural images of prophet, priest, and sage and the basic tenets of three models of interdisciplinary work in practical theology furnish an intellectually robust, holistic, and constructive theological hermeneutic for contemporary preaching?" On the one hand, Gilbert argues that a homiletical theology (or theological hermeneutic) of promise must be viewed in context and in light of broader goals: "its fundamental aim is to beckon postmodern preachers to preach the whole counsel of Scripture, proclaiming the promises of God in light of the principles of divine justice, spiritual transformation, and realistic hope." On the other hand, Gilbert's vision remains an expansive, global one. The language of promise is a means by which a more global homiletical-theological vision may ensue, one connected deeply to philosopher Josiah Royce's notion of the "beloved community." Such community, says Gilbert is not about forming theological consensus, but building relationship.

The next two chapters take a slightly different turn. These two chapters seek to broaden notions of homiletical theology into different "intersections" and "forms" as described above.

In chapter 3, Ruthanna Hooke brings homiletical theology into deeper dialogue with a liturgical theology by means of the embodied practice of preaching. Her article, "The Spirit-Breathed Body: Divine Presence and Eschatological Promise in Preaching," compares the role of the Spirit in preaching to the epiclesis of the Eucharist. Drawing on the embodied perspective of performance in the Linklater school of voice in the dramatic arts, Hooke explores the homiletical-theological intersection of a theology of preaching as a means of deepening an understanding of promise through the bodily breathing and speaking of the preacher. Following the distinction between primary and secondary theology among liturgical theologians, Hooke theologizes the breath and voice of the preacher in deep sacramental connection with the Spirit. "If preaching is sacramental, is it possible to locate an *epiclesis* in the preaching event? I suggest that the *epiclesis* in the Eucharist is analogous to the preacher's moment-by-moment experience of the breath in the body." What results is a unique challenge to a homiletical theology of promise to push beyond concerns with contextual theologies of the gospel to deepened theologies of preaching that press toward a more embodied homiletical theology of promise.

Paul Wilson likewise presses a homiletical theology of promise in a different direction—not so much in terms of its "intersections," as with Hooke, but in terms of its type. In his chapter, "A Homiletical Theology of Promise: More Than One Genre?" Wilson raises the question not so much at the form or level of homiletical theology (as in Bartow's distinctions between scholarly, professional, and pedagogical), but in terms of its genre or shape in writing and speech. Wilson begins by recounting the importance of promise in Biblical witness and thus offers an important orienting vision in his essay for the whole consultation's work. At the same time, Wilson also points out that the means of doing so is not marked by the generic features of the scholarly paper, but by the poetic language of preaching itself. What Wilson envisions is a kind of third way of doing homiletical theologically, generically speaking, somewhere between the sermon and the scholarly article. His concern is that homiletical theology not lose its roots in the poetry of promise itself.

The final two chapters then seek to relate a homiletical theology of promise to close and sometimes revisionist readings of theologies of promise born in white, Euro-American traditions. Here the language of promise finds its roots especially in the Reformation and theological reflection that emerges out of that into twentieth- and twenty-first -century re-contextualizations. An important thing to note: despite the historic hegemony of such Euro-American traditions and their pretension to a-contextuality, even here promise and context interact in deep and surprising ways.

In chapter 5, James Kay retrieves a notion of the gospel as promise and shows its surprising, deep connection to context in the work of Rudolf Bultmann in Kay's article "Promissory Kerygmatics." The language of kerygmatics, of course, is usually linked to an understanding of promise that moves decisively "down-hill" from divine revelation to human life. The goal of considering how a core sense of the gospel's character as promise in relation to context would seem beyond reach in neo-orthodox traditions. Nonetheless, Kay invites readers to reconsider Bultmann's notion of *Entweltlichung* (freedom from the world *and* freedom for the world) as both a powerful form of counter-cultural contextualization and as a kind of "countersign," especially in relation to the struggles over white racism, sexism, and anti-immigrant ethnocentrism in the contemporary context. Just as Bultmann's notion of *Entweltlichung* offered space for Bultmann's promise-oriented understanding of the gospel to ground resistance to National Socialism in Germany, so also a retrieved notion of *Entweltlichung* offers a surprising vista for holding to contextualizations and engagement of promise in our troubled times today. The result is a holding together of gospel promise and context that brings together strands of divine grace/presence and justice.

In the final chapter, I offer a revisionist reading of Luther's understanding of promise for a twenty-first-century context in the white, mainline church: "Promise as an Event of the Gospel in Context: Toward an Unfinished Homiletical Theology of Grace and Justice." This article envisions a homiletical theology of promise in context as a faithful, praxis-oriented theological enterprise that holds together God's grace and God's justice as an unfolding mystery in *Anfechtung* or struggle. It draws chiefly on Luther's traditions of what "makes a good theologian," God hidden and revealed, as well as God preached and not preached—all as mediated through Oswald Bayer's theology of promise and lament in relation to Austin's speech act theory. Like Bayer's work, this essay takes seriously the idea that promise is "undergone" in *Anfechtung*, here understood to include suffering, struggle, and ecclesial *praxis*. In this way, the essay here departs from Bayer's position by arguing that the relationship of theory and praxis in preaching promise is understood not solely in relation to the *vita passiva*, but an event in context that involves what philosopher Hannah Arendt calls the *vita activa* with respect to promise and provisional public action.

CONCLUSION

The essays in this volume may discuss promise as a homiletical-theological concern, but they also bear together unique witness to the vibrancy of promise across and within traditions. The point of this final volume is not to catalogue the whole lot, but to open the door to an ever widening-conversation about promise at the heart of the task of preaching. As homiletician Kenyatta Gilbert argues, the conversation around promise holds the potential for generating wider conversations in Josiah Royce's "beloved community," a place, perhaps, where promises are not only named but also redeemed in the give and take of different cultural traditions—and ultimately, I would argue, with respect to Christ in whom "every one of God's promises is a 'Yes.'" (2 Cor 1:20b).

— 1 —

The Promised Land
A Postcolonial Homiletic of Promise in the Asian American Context

—Sunggu Yang

INTRODUCTION

At the core of Asian American preaching is the promise of the Promised Land.[1] This thesis I base on the fact that over the past century Asian Americans[2] have constructed their unique faith deeply rooted in the *lim-*

---

1. Throughout the article, the Promised Land appears as capitalized in most cases in order to show the uniqueness of that idea in the Christian tradition and its significant theological weight in the Asian American ecclesial context. For the reason for the seemingly tautological designation of this phrase, see the Conclusion.

2. Asian Americans today represent a wide range of Asian North American groups: that is, East Asian Americans (e.g., Chinese, Japanese, and Korean Americans), South Asian Americans (e.g., Indian, Nepali, and Pakistani Americans), Southeast Asian Americans (e.g., Filipino, Malaysian, and Vietnamese Americans), and Pacific Islanders as well. This essay dares not discuss a broad spectrum of Christian spirituality or practices in faith from all different Asian ethnic groups, but instead focuses on East Asian American spirituality and its preaching practice. For East Asian Christianity is still a major player in Asian North America when it comes to spiritual influence, theological development, Christian practice, and missional energy. Research on other groups, I hope, shall follow in the future as their presence in and impact on Asian American Christianity grows. Also, when I use the term Asian American in my research, I mainly refer to first generation Asians who, though still fundamentally Asian by culture, have adopted an Americanized way of life and mostly tend to live in America for good. They are still mother-tongue

inal experience of living in a foreign land as a marginalized stranger or a "pilgrim."³ In other words, the immigrant's spiritual experience of pilgrimage, as the perpetual sojourner walking in a strange world and looking forward to another (heavenly) world, determines the constructs of faith. The metaphoric idea or the promise of the Promised Land best represents the other heavenly reality that Asian Americans perceive as the eventual terminal of their spiritual pilgrimage. What is important here is that the idea or perceived reality of the Promised Land is not really ethereal or purely other-worldly. Rather, the desired Promised Land synthesizes this-worldliness and other-worldliness. That is, Asian Americans see the Promised Land as already being established here on American soil, yet as also having an eschatological prospect. Preaching, as the most significant moment in the weekly liturgy and spiritual life of the Asian American ecclesia,⁴ concretizes the synthetic message of the Promised Land in the most verbal and explicit sense, as I will show through examples from Eunjoo Kim's sermons toward the end of the chapter.

The main body of my article begins by investigating the socio-ecclesial context of Asian Americans, whose pilgrim identity is born out of their triple consciousness. Then, the article discusses the biblical (specifically, Abrahamic) and Augustinian traditions of the pilgrim spirituality that Asian Americans

---

speaking adults with English as their second language. As is well-known, second and third generation Asian Americans—the US-born and raised—have their particular cultural and theological perspectives and stories. Investigating this latter group's socio-ecclesial natures and homiletic practice is simply beyond the scope of this study.

3. Sang Hyun Lee adopts British anthropologist Victor Turner's term, "liminality," in order to articulate the cultural "in-between" phenomenon or experience of the Asian American immigrants. Lee, *From a Liminal Place*, 4–11; cf. Turner, *Ritual Process*, 94ff. Lee argues that Asian Americans living "at the edge of America and also between America and Asia are placed in a liminal space . . . where a person is freed up from the usual ways of thinking and acting and is therefore open to radically new ideas." And he continues, "Freed from structure, persons in liminality are also available to a genuine communion (*communitas*) with others." Lee believes that this liminal experience of the immigrant status has significantly influenced immigrant life in general and the immigrant person's faith formation in particular. As we shall see later, based on this liminality idea, Lee suggests his creative Asian American Christian understanding of the immigrant life—the metaphoric image of the pilgrim, which is widely accepted in the Asian American socio-ecclesial context.

4. For instance, Jung Young Lee writes regarding this central position of preaching in the Korean American worship, "In fact, preaching is *more than merely a part of the worship service; it is, in fact, a worship service*. Every act of worship can be regarded as preaching. Prayers, music, hymn singing, reading scriptures, the citation of creeds, and the attitude of a congregation are all forms of preaching. Each action conveys the Word of God in its own form and style (emphasis inserted)." Jung Young Lee, *Korean Preaching*, 41.

have adopted and adapted for their own context. Finally, I detail the Promised Land idea/ideal and the resulting Asian American pilgrim homiletic of promise. Though not explicit, the overall tone of the article is postcolonial, something that is inevitable given that a significant part of Asian American theological thought is an attempt to overcome their colonial experience, either geo-politically or spiritually. Yet, any discussion on postcolonial theology itself will remain in the background, given the article's focus on pilgrim theology and the idea of the Promised Land.[5]

SOCIO-THEOLOGICAL CONTEXT: THE TRIPLE CONSCIOUSNESS OF ASIAN AMERICAN CHRISTIANS[6]

Asian American Christians, as this socio-religious designation of them itself indicates, live in a threefold cultural-religious reality as *Asian, American,* and *Christian.* To adopt and adapt W. E. B. Du Bois' argument and terminology, Asian Americans construct their identity by means of *triple consciousness.* Du Bois once argued that African Americans live a "double consciousness" due to two predominant social and existential realities of being African and American. They oscillate between these often-conflicting identities, "two souls, two thoughts, two unreconciled strivings," at times confused by and at times benefitting from double consciousness.[7] Yet Du Bois realized that double consciousness itself is a thing to overcome, not something to be endured helplessly or to be purposefully appropriated. Thus, he argued for the creation of a holistic self-consciousness, self-realization, and self-respect beyond the tricky double consciousness in the minds of African Americans. Building on Du Bois' argument, I therefore note that Asian American Christians have a triple consciousness: as Asian, as American, and as Christian, or specifically Christ-believing and Christ-following.[8] Yet for Asian Americans, in contrast

---

5. Some minor portions of this article are modified renditions from my previous research with a new topical angle of the Promised Land. In particular, for a full exploration of biblical-theological and cultural foundations of the pilgrim and the Promised Land ideas in the Asian American context, refer to Chapter One of my recent publication, *Evangelical Pilgrims from the East,* 2016.

6. For a deeper analysis of the Asian American socio-ecclesial context, see ibid., 2–11.

7. Du Bois et al., *The Souls of Black Folk Essays and Sketches,* 17.

8. As well-known, Asian American Christian life is highly Christo-centric, whether one has conservative or progressive faith orientation. In conservative circles, Christo-centric faith takes a form of Christian exclusivism (i.e., Jesus, the only savior of the sinful world) while the same faith provides a foundation of liberative theology (i.e., Jesus, the prototype of the religio-social revolutionary) for the progressives. In this article, I use

to African Americans, these three fundamentals of socio-religious consciousness do not necessarily contradict one another. Rather, Asian Americans find that being *triple-minded* is necessary for their survival. Specifically, their initial identity as Asian (or being a part of the Asian community) is crucial for their communal survival in a hostile foreign land, while a new identity as American is also essential for their daily socio-economic lives. At the same time, living as Christ-believing serves them as the most fundamental spiritual resolution to the inevitable psychological, social, economic, or political conflicts that stem from being both Asian and American. In what follows, Sang Hyun Lee, Matsuoka Fumitaka, and Kwok Pui-lan each articulate how this triple consciousness plays out richly in the Asian American Christian life.

In his *From a Liminal Place: An Asian American Theology*, Sang Hyun Lee first presents his theological analysis of the Asian American social context, especially its bicultural nature. Two concepts are significant in his writing: *liminality* and *marginality*. Asian Americans live a liminal life between two very different cultures, which makes their social status extremely marginalized from both cultures; that is, they do not and cannot truly belong to either of the two cultures, and thus are aliens to both. However, Lee is not pessimistic. Based on symbolic anthropologist Victor Turner's positive conception of liminality, Lee contends that being situated in two different cultures is a profound and complex experience in which new and creative possibilities of life are born.[9] Lee believes in particular that this experience of cultural liminality in the Asian American context can produce three invaluable benefits: 1) openness to the new or hidden potentials of society, 2) the emergence of *communitas*, and 3) a creative space for prophetic knowledge and subversive action.[10] Lee's belief is that Christ, himself a person from the social margins who once lived a liminal life between two sets of dualistic worlds (i.e., human and heavenly *and* Jewish and Greco-Roman), is the best model for the people of God of a person who (has) achieved the above threefold benefit. Then, Jesus-believing and Jesus-following becomes the third quintessential

Jesus and Christ as totally interchangeable terms with no doctrinal or historical specifications attached to them.

9. Lee, *From a Liminal Place*, 1–6.

10. Ibid., 7–11. Lee realizes that since Asian American Christians live in this unstructured, open-ended liminal space, they have a certain potential to come up with very new spiritual ideas, social structures, and cultural expressions that can contribute to the breadth, depth, and width of the existing society's cultural life. Besides, these new hybrid Asian American Christians can help the emergence of *communitas* where people from all racial and ethnic groups would, together, create a community of harmony, justice, and peace. Last, but not least, thanks to the freedom from and critical response to the existing social structure, the Asian American Christians living through liminality could possibly serve as the prophetic agents of God vis-à-vis the oft-unjust dominant culture.

socio-religious consciousness of Asian Americans. That is, *being Christian* is a third ontological foundation for Asian Americans, along with *being Asian* and *being American.*

While agreeing on Lee's arguments on liminality and Christian faith as a core ontological foundation of the Asian American life, Fumitaka Matsuoka in his *Out of Silence: Emerging Themes in Asian American Churches* calls for active social activism by Asian American Christians. He acknowledges that the Asian American church historically has served two socio-ecclesial functions for the people who are part of it. First, the church has been the reservoir of an original Asian cultural and linguistic heritage. In church, people celebrate their own culture and practice their own language that, outside of the church, cannot be celebrated or practiced fully. Second, the church has helped the people's cultural integration into American society and the local community, providing necessary physical/emotional and economic help.[11] Though Matsuoka finds these two social functions very helpful and necessary, he suggests they are insufficient, for they are too passive to make real social or spiritual changes in or out of the Asian American church, in the light of the larger American society. Because of their "ghettoization," Asian American Christians specifically and Asian Americans in general have been silent or silenced in the broader dominant and colonizing culture. Matsuoka encourages the church to get out of its own ethnic and cultural enclave in order: 1) to demonstrate the church's legitimate social place in the wider society, and 2) more importantly, to envision and strive to achieve a new American social reality of racial reconciliation, political equality, and socio-economic justice based on the lessons of Christian scriptures and the liberative message of Christ. Matsuoka agrees with Lee that Asian Americans can envision this new kind of transformed American reality because they are now living in the creative space of the "state of liminality."[12] That is, although Asian Americans seem to live in a fixed marginal reality defined by the powerful dominant culture, they are extremely open to new ideas, particularly ideas based on the vision of the Kingdom of God that could possibly transform American society.[13] As is the case with Lee, so too Matsuoka is optimistic about the power and authority of the Christian faith in Christ the Incarnate, who once served and still serves his people in concrete human history as a realistic hope for the broken world.[14]

It should be noted that in their triple consciousness-based optimism or ideal of egalitarian *communitas* or the transformed American reality, Lee and

11. Matsuoka, *Out of Silence*, 13–15.
12. Ibid., 61.
13. Ibid., 61–63.
14. Ibid., 31.

Matsuoka do not hold up Asian Americans as the best sole task force to be utilized, however they may be effective or powerful. It will be simply too much for Asian Americans, still marginalized and forced to be in society, to take up the transformative task alone. The transformative and reconciliatory task, Lee and Matsuoka contend therefore, must be carried out by firmly establishing "solidarity" and "mutual interdependence" with *others* around them for synergic cooperative impact.[15] Asian Americans can serve as initiators of that synergic impact with their fresh insights from the (positive) margins.

Postcolonial feminist theologian Kwok Pui-lan speaks further about Asian American life and triple consciousness from her own daily experience of "diasporic existence."[16] She finds herself in limbo or in the liminality between being Asian and American, yet more specifically between once-colonized Asia and colonizing America, and particularly so as a woman of color whose existence in North America is another form of marginalization. Kwok knows that she is not the only woman in this doubly vulnerable colonial-racist context. In fact most Asian American women share this predicament. Her audacious resolution for this perilous situation is a third way of postcolonial feminist theology. This theology, often Christological, is a third way since it moves beyond the dualism of colonized (i.e., Asian) and colonizing (i.e., Euro-American) and, more important, seeks the liberation of Asian American women beyond white-male dominant colonial subjugation and violent racial conflicts (e.g., white males' dominant power over Asian American women's lives and their hyper-sexualized bodies). Therefore, she contends that a primary task of Asian American Christians is the practice of postcolonial feminist imagination or the claim of "the Third Space" to borrow Christopher Baker and Homi Bhabha's terminology.[17]

---

15. Ibid., 112 and S. Lee, *From a Liminal Place*, 153.

16. Kwok, *Postcolonial Imagination and Feminist Theology*, 25.

17. Baker, *The Hybrid Church in the City*, 16. The Third Space is a metaphor for the Christian church's work by which the social or religious status quo is deconstructed and a new communal hope and reality is implanted. This Third Space work is not of a "once-and-for-all" nature but should be continually renewed; Kwok, "Postcolonial Preaching in Intercultural Contexts," 9–10. Homi Bhabha originally coined the term *third space* in connection with his postcolonial notion of *hybridity*. He notices that people oscillating between the colonizer's hegemonic-cultural authority and the person's initial cultural orientation come to formulate a hybrid identity that is very new to the former two though emerging and taking certain characteristics from the two. This new hybrid identity appears as disruption and displacement of the existing colonial powers which cannot fully grasp the new cultural thrust and creativity of people's hybridity and thus dismiss it by their typical universal cultural claims. Translated politically or sociologically, this hybrid people become a key source of protest, subversion, reconstruction, and of colonial-hegemonic society. Where the existing-exclusive colonial status quo is subverted, the people of hybrid identity newly create the more inclusive third space that "initiates new signs of

In sum, the eventual goal of Lee, Fumitaka, and Kwok is the same though each one proposes different nuances and foci for this goal of people discovering and adopting a third consciousness of the Asian American life through faith in Christ, the true liberator, transformer, and reconciler. This third consciousness, and thus *triple consciousness*, generates a unique Asian American Christian faith that is beneficial not only for Asian Americans but also for all Americans, in that its goal is ultimately reconciliation between the two. What is more significant and insightful for our discussion is that faith in Christ enables Asian Americans to envision a third liberative reality as the eventual destination of their faithful lives and the ultimate transformation of the current hostile foreign land.

How does this liberating and transformative triple consciousness actually play out in the daily and weekly spiritual lives of Asian Americans, especially in the practice of preaching? The idea of being a pilgrim journeying toward the Promised Land is central, for it promises *something more and something greater* than what Asian Americans encounter in this heart-crushing foreign land.

METAPHORS OF THE PILGRIM AND THE PROMISED LAND: THE BIBLE AND AUGUSTINE

As we will see in the next sections, because the metaphoric ideas of the pilgrim and the Promised Land prevail in Asian American spirituality and thus in the practice of preaching, so too do they pervade triple consciousness. Where does the idea or ideal of the pilgrim journeying toward the Promised Land originate? Among numerous sources, the Abrahamic story from the Hebrew Bible and St. Augustine's pilgrim theology are primary and are two sources that Asian Americans have adopted and adapted for their own use.[18]

From the beginning of Genesis through the end of Revelation, the themes of pilgrimage and of the Promised Land represent core theological

---

identity, and innovative sites of collaboration and contestation." In short, hybrid people convey a considerable potential to become a counter-hegemonic agent and startling (or "shocking" to the colonial authorities) socio-political innovator. Bhabha, *The Location of Culture*, 1; "Frontlines/Borderposts," 269–72; "Cultures in Between."

18. It is commonly known and accepted that St. Augustine's political thoughts and pilgrim ideal have deeply penetrated spirituality, theology, and ethics of the Korean church since its missional inception. Jiwhang Lew, among many, provides a persuasive account regarding how St. Augustine's pilgrim ideal has (re)directed the Korean church's self-identity as an ethical and political agency in society. In particular, Lew acknowledges the pilgrim life as one's socio-ethical response to God's love to the world (or to sinners). Lew, "Politics of Virtue," and his "The Korean Church as a Polis," 324–47.

understandings of humanity and earthly life.[19] The Genesis account narrates the story of paradise lost, in which the first human beings are thrown into the earthly wilderness, or "exile" as Dee Dyas calls it,[20] where they are to "till the ground from which [they were] taken."[21] As the continuing account of Genesis recalls, however, the exiled humans are not completely alone in their wilderness. Not only does God prepare garments to clothe Adam and Eve, but that God still cares for fallen humanity is something that their offspring through the generations do not forget as they "invoke the name of the Lord."[22] Yet, notwithstanding God's care and love, humanity lives outside paradise and is on a life-time pilgrimage toward that now lost perfect reality. Many generations later, the prophet Isaiah dreams of a recovered paradise or the Promised Land in which "[t]he wolf and the lamb shall feed together, the lion shall eat straw like the ox; but the serpent—its food shall be dust! They shall not hurt or destroy on all my holy mountain, says the Lord."[23] This specific quotation from Isaiah, though not really about a fundamental human yearning toward paradise lost, nonetheless recalls his once-ruined nation's historically recovered future. Here Isaiah uses eschatological language in order to point out his nation's, and indeed all humanity's, deviation from God and the resulting disharmony that can only be perfectly restored on the Last Day. Until then, we will continue on our inevitable spiritual journey, yearning for that other perfect and harmonious world.

Genesis 12, specifically Abraham's story of sojourning to another land, reflects the pervasive theme of spiritual pilgrimage.[24] On the surface, the story seems to be about a faithful person's historical or mythic immigration to a foreign yet promised land in his obedience to Yahweh. However, on a symbolic, theological level, as Dyas points out, this story also serves as a very strong representation of all humanity's lifetime pilgrimage to a reality prepared by God that is to be experienced beyond human history.[25] We see this theme of

---

19. Three authors, McConville, Lincoln, and Motyer each investigate pilgrimage as it appears respectively in the Hebrew Bible, the New Testament, and Pauline writings. See chapters 2–4 in *Explorations in Christian Theology of Pilgrimage*.

20. Dyas, *Pilgrimage in Medieval English Literature, 700–1500*, 14.

21. Gen 3:23 (all biblical quotations from NRSV throughout the article).

22. Gen 4:26b.

23. Isa 65:25.

24. Dyas, *Pilgrimage in Medieval English Literature*, 15–16. See also "Exile and Pilgrimage," 254–59. He notes, "The motif of the faithful servant of God as a pilgrim for whom this world is not his final home is deeply rooted in the exilic narratives of Genesis (the calling of Abraham) and Exodus."

25. Dyas, *Pilgrimage in Medieval English Literature*, 15–16.

lifetime pilgrimage intensified in the intra-textual and allegorical interpretation of the Abrahamic event in the Book of Hebrews:

> By faith Abraham obeyed when he was called to set out for a place that he was to receive as an inheritance; and he set out, not knowing where he was going. By faith he stayed for a time *in the land he had been promised*, as in a foreign land, living in tents, as did Isaac and Jacob, who were heirs with him of the same promise. For he looked forward to the city that has foundations, whose *architect and builder is God* . . . All of these died in faith without having received the promises, but from a distance they saw and greeted them. They confessed that they were strangers and foreigners on the earth, for people who speak in this way make it clear that they are seeking a homeland. If they had been thinking of the land that they had left behind, they would have had opportunity to return. But as it is, they desire a better country, that is, *a heavenly one*. Therefore God is not ashamed to be called their God; indeed, [God] has prepared a city for them. (Hebrews 11:8–10, 13–16; emphases mine)

What this passage clearly demonstrates is that Abraham lived on the earth as a stranger or pilgrim, and had a desire for a better homeland, a heavenly one, whose architect is none other than God. The writer of Hebrews has no hesitation in calling Abraham the biblical model of a lifetime pilgrim journeying in a strange land toward a promised one. The eyes of the writer are largely focused on the *other* reality, namely the Promised Land.

Augustine further developed the spirituality of the Abrahamic pilgrimage that conveys explicit ethical claims "during the journey" before getting to the promised one. Mary T. Clark acknowledges that Augustine's spirituality is the spirituality of pilgrimage imbued with images of wilderness, paradise, exiles, repatriation, promised land, etc.[26] If we understand his *Confessions* as his own "odyssey of soul,"[27] we see that Augustine narrates his personal life story as a journey from bondage or exile of the soul to a liberating state of absolute and infinite good.[28] Of this, Augustine writes: "I shall go into my own little

---

26. Introduction, in Clark, *Augustine of Hippo*, 42.

27. O'Connell's interpretation of Augustine's spirituality in *Confessions* in his *St. Augustine's Confessions*.

28. Augustine and Chadwick, *Confessions*, XII, 16. However, this kind of transitory theology for "that which is above" is not always favored among Christians. Some critics, such as Craig G. Bartholomew, accuse Augustine of hyper-privileging that which is above in his theology based on Neoplatonism. Bartholomew, *Where Mortals Dwell*, 202. In a similar vein, Dietrich Bonhoeffer once said, "[I]t was a near catastrophe for Christianity when it became more closely related to Neoplatonism than to Old Testament realism."

room and sing love songs to Thee, groaning unutterable groanings during my pilgrimage, recalling in my heart the Jerusalem to which my heart has been uplifted, Jerusalem my home, Jerusalem my mother."[29] Augustine acknowledges that the gift of God or the Holy Spirit kindles genuine love for God in his heart, which will eventually lead him to his "home Jerusalem" where he will want to remain forever. Until he reaches that final destination, he will reside in this world as a pilgrim still tempted by worldly desires. Augustine wants to inform us that his confession on the spiritual journey, though personal, yet applies to all other fellow human beings as a universal spiritual phenomenon.

Just a decade or so after the completion of *Confessions*, Augustine had another opportunity to address this pilgrim identity of humankind for the general public. In his *The City of God against the Pagans*, it is obvious that his eyes are firmly fixed on Heaven once again. What is notable this time around is that his pilgrim spirituality does not seem to be universal anymore. Rather, the pilgrim journey is restricted only to Christians who wander the earth "on pilgrimage in this mortal state."[30] Those on the pilgrim journey will be tempted by worldly pleasures, and thus some return to the City of Man that is doomed to eventual destruction on the Last Day. Yet, those who keep walking the pilgrimage way will taste "the perfectly ordered and completely harmonious fellowship in the enjoyment of God, and of each other in God."[31] This enjoyment of God or "the [heavenly] peace," however, does not mean that the Christian pilgrims now (must) live "above" or "out of" the world. On the contrary, their lives are very much bound to the City of Man; there is no immediate escape. Indeed, this is why they are called to be *pilgrims and not angels* in heaven. Augustine further argues that this earth-bound life of the pilgrim demands a missionary or ethical (or righteous) life style and attitude. Simply put, the heaven-bound pilgrims must differentiate themselves from those who are bound to the sinful, decaying City of Man so that: 1) Christians, by the example of their good lives, might save some others by the grace of God; and, more importantly, 2) they might not be tempted again into the worldly way of life.[32]

This *missional-ethical* dimension of the pilgrim life is Augustine's creative development, though not unique to him; a similar idea already appears in the biblical-theological understanding of pilgrimage. However, while the latter focuses more on the dimension of the *spiritual purity* that distinguishes

Dumas, *Dietrich Bonhoeffer, Theologian of Reality*, 153.
29. Augustine, *City of God*, XII, 16.
30. Ibid., XVIII, 32.
31. Ibid., XIX, 17.
32. Ibid.

pilgrims from the sinful world, Augustine emphasizes the *spiritual fruits* of those pilgrims, fruits that they bear on their heaven-bound journey *here on the earth*. Thus, it is no wonder when Augustine admonishes his fellow Christians, saying, "[On your journey] do no harm to anyone" and "help anyone whenever possible."[33] For him, it is obvious that the "faith [of the pilgrim must be] put into action by love."[34] Yet, pilgrim Christians are not to dream of a perfectly restored world made possible by their ethical action in love. The City of Man is ultimately bound to the eternal death. There is no conclusive salvation for it, and pilgrims are not here to save that sinful world, apparently. What pilgrim Christians can only hope for, Augustine realizes, is the faithful missional-ethical demonstration of what is coming on the Last Judgment Day and their patient journey to the heavenly, Promised Land; until then, thankfully, we are called to live "in the enjoyment of God, and of each other in God."[35]

Both the Abrahamic account and the pilgrim idea of Augustine describe the Christian life as a continuing journey toward the Promised Land. The journey itself is the covenantal promise of God that is unbreakable. Augustine, however, expresses a somewhat stronger missional-ethical dimension of the pilgrim journey even though his eyes are fixed more on the ethereal, heaven-bound reality that is to come later.

As I discuss below, Asian Americans have adopted and adapted the pilgrim theology and the Promised Land ethos from both the biblical-Abrahamic and the Augustinian accounts in a way that best addresses their own socio-theological context. In particular, we will see that in the Asian American context the Promised Land now conveys a dual meaning, namely, of something that is *already but not yet*, a more radical development from Augustine.

PILGRIMAGE AND THE PROMISED LAND IN THE ASIAN AMERICAN CONTEXT

The triple consciousness of Asian Americans has led them to look for the unique *third socio-religious identity* that goes beyond being *Asian* and *American* and also overcomes the inevitable marginality imposed by their bicultural life. At the core of their new identity are the ideas of the pilgrim and the Promised Land rooted in the biblical (especially the Abrahamic story) and

---

33. Ibid., XIX, 14.
34. Ibid.
35. Ibid., XIX, 17.

Augustinian theological accounts.³⁶ Below, I explore in detail useful arguments from Lee and Fumitaka in regards to the further development of the pilgrim and the Promised Land ideas in the Asian American context, namely, the socio-religious synthesis of *this-earthliness* and *other-worldliness*.

Lee sees the Abrahamic story and other similar Bible narratives of pilgrimage, combined together, as *the* narrative(s) upon which Asian American Christians have constructed their own version of the "pilgrimage-in-the-wilderness" spirituality.³⁷ Perceiving their new socio-geographic location in the United States as their own wilderness, Asian American Christians have created their own particular bicultural theological and ontological narrative ground. In a spiritual-symbolic sense, they now find the same wilderness in which Adam and Eve, Abraham, the ancient Israelites, and other faithful Christians would have walked in their own pilgrim journeys. Lee writes, "The Abrahamic obedience to God's call has been invoked in the Asian American church. The challenge is to see the Asian immigrants' de facto uprootedness as an opportunity to embark on a sacred pilgrimage to some God-promised [Land], and therefore to believe that life as strangers and exiles can be meaningful."³⁸

What is particularly interesting in Lee's development of the pilgrim and the Promised Land ideas is the strong synthesis of *this-earthliness* and *other-worldliness*; in other terms, a synthesis of social-liberative vision and eschatological hope. For Lee, the earthly wilderness on which Asian Americans journey is not to remain the wilderness forever. As they progress on their pilgrim journey, the exilic strange land where marginalization is considered "normal" will go through transformation envisioned in the hope of the ultimate Promised Land. In other words, the other-worldly Promised Land is being implanted *already here and now*. This is the real vocation of the Christian pilgrim as well as the valid promise of *Christ-Once-Marginalized-Yet-Exalted* contextually given to Asian Americans. Thus, Lee continues:

> That the exalted Jesus is with us also can only mean that the community of Jesus which is still on earth has an eternal dimension; Jesus' community is tied up permanently with the exalted head of that community. The seemingly fragile community of consciously liminal and marginalized Asian American followers of Jesus has

---

36. Asian American scholars find that the theological motif of pilgrimage or life as spiritual journey is shared extensively among most Asian American ethnic groups. For a detailed discussion, see Nagano, "A Japanese American Pilgrimage," 63–79; Ng, *People on the Way*, xv–xxix; Das, "Sojourners in the Land of the Free," 19–34; and Choy, "Strangers Called to Mission," 65–89.

37. Lee, "Pilgrimage and Home in the Wilderness of Marginality," 61.

38. Lee, *From a Liminal Place*, 4–11, 61–64.

the exalted Lord as its head and leader. This tie of the Asian American church with the exalted Lord is this eschatological future and divinely guaranteed promise. And that promise is the source of Asian American believers' courage to live in awareness of their liminal space and the source of endurance in their struggle against marginalization.[39]

Lee then makes another radical statement about this transformational potential and power of Asian American pilgrims, with an Abrahamic-eschatological prospect:

> Abraham's story is particularly pertinent to Asian immigrants who may be wondering what the meaning of their existence in this country is. Abraham's story can be interpreted as saying that now that the Asian immigrants have left home and are here in America, it is an opportunity to take up the pilgrimage toward a "better America" and work to make America a country that is more according to God's will. Their situation can be seen as a calling to live as the creative minority in America. Moreover, if Asian Christians appropriate Abraham's story as their own, they might see their life's goal as being to continue to live here "as strangers and foreigners" and work to build a "better America," "whose architect and builder is God." In this way, their Christian faith would have something to do with their identity and their life as marginalized and liminal people in America.[40]

Fumitaka echoes Lee's theme of "pilgrimage-in-the-wilderness" when he acknowledges Asian American Christians as "strangers and sojourners" living in the household of God. In this foreign yet promised land, he realizes, Asian Americans have been always "on the way," not belonging to either Asia or America, but to the liminal space where their Christian faith helps them envision a new reality of America.[41] Fumitaka in particular encourages Asian Americans to envision and strive to achieve a new American social reality of racial reconciliation, political equality, and socio-economic justice from their fresh marginal perspective of the world. In that respect, just as Lee articulates above, Fumitaka perceives *the Asian American pilgrim life in the spiritual wilderness* as a positive ontological-communal narrative and highly meaningful in a synthetic-eschatological sense, though he is fully aware of its limitations

---

39. Ibid., 87.
40. Ibid., 122.
41. Matsuoka, *Out of Silence*, 1, 9, 31.

as well.[42] In agreement with Lee and Fumitaka, and so also with the Abrahamic pilgrimage ethos, Wesley Woo, Chinese American pastor and scholar, states confessionally:

> We still are a pursuing church, or the pilgrim of God in the Wilderness... [W]e are all on the way, together. But we are not alone, nor helpless. Our fathers [and mothers] crossed over the Pacific for a new life in this [Promised Land]. They found what the life of sojourners was like, and yet, wherever they were, they were not away from the Lord's field. They met him, and built their churches.[43]

In sum, Asian Americans have adopted and adapted the Abrahamic pilgrimage narrative in a typological sense and promoted it to a highly eschatological level that specifically addresses their unique socio-cultural context. At the same time, in a synthetic sense they have "brought down" the same eschatological promise of God—the Promised Land—to the "dusty earth" so that God's promise executes its transformative spirit and power here and now in the American wilderness. Thus, the Augustinian ethical claims on the Christian pilgrim life take on more significance or ultimate significance in the Asian American pilgrim life.

Asian American preachers have been quick to adopt and apply in their preaching this synthetic *already-but-not-yet* spirituality of the Promised Land that prevails in their congregational context. Thus, as I discuss in detail in the following section, their message is bold enough to proclaim the Promised Land (e.g., a transformed postcolonial American reality) being *already* implanted during the Asian American pilgrim journey, *yet* it also recognizes that their journey must go on because the ultimate Promised Land is awaiting them at the end of their life-long pilgrimage. There, at the final moment, they will no longer be called either Asian American or pilgrims, but will be embraced only as equal children of God along with all others.

THE PROMISED LAND: A SYNTHETIC MESSAGE OF PROMISE FROM THE PILGRIM PREACHER

We're pilgrims called by God
to continue struggling

---

42. Ibid., 13–15. Here, Fumitaka points out the "ghetto" phenomenon of the Asian American church, which significantly contributed to Asian Americans being silent or silenced, in the broader culture.

43. Woo, "Asians in America," 20.

until the day when all immigrant people,
not only [Asians] but also other ethnic groups,
fully belong to this new land
and equally inherit this promised land of God.[44]

This sermon excerpt from Eunjoo Kim is a fine example of the synthetic message of promise by the Asian American pilgrim preacher. Kim is proclaiming God's eschatological promise (i.e., the Promised Land) "brought down" to American soil for the sake of all children of God. That is, as a preacher Kim *is already seeing* God's promise being achieved for all pilgrims of God in her very *Sitz im Leben*. In this respect, the Promised Land is the exact synonym of the ultimate promise that the Asian American pilgrim preacher can provide for her fellow pilgrims in their wilderness journey. In short, at the core of the pilgrim preacher's sermonic message is always the promise that the Promised Land is being realized *today*.

Here one cannot miss the significance and legitimacy of the term *promise* that is adopted homiletically by the Asian American pilgrim preacher. In this context, the word "promise" conveys far more than do words like "vision" or "hope." *The Oxford Dictionary* defines promise as "A declaration or assurance that one will do something or that a particular thing will happen." The same dictionary defines hope as "a feeling of expectation and desire for a particular thing to happen" and vision as "the ability to think about or plan the future with imagination or wisdom."[45] What the Asian American pilgrim preacher proclaims (as Kim's example shows) is an unequivocal declaration and assurance that the Promised Land will happen (indeed is happening in the present!), but is *detectable* if only we have pilgrim eyes to see it. The ongoing realization of the Promised Land is neither a good "feeling of expectation and desire" for the Promised Land to happen nor a fine future plan full of "imagination or wisdom," even though those understandings are not entirely excluded. In short, the preacher's message is declaration, that is, promise being executed readily, solemnly, and eschatologically. This is why Jung Young Lee's sermon below may sound familiar and sweet to Asian Americans' ears:

> Pioneers are people who don't go back to their homeland when they face problems and troubles in the new land. Pioneers are those who have made up their minds to stay for good in the new land. They have the faith of Abraham. They are not conformists but cultivators of a new land. We have to cultivate the wilderness if we are pioneers. Our wilderness is a society of injustice and prejudice,

---

44. Kim, *Preaching the Presence of God*, 158.

45. See the terms "promise," "vision," and "hope" at http://www.oxforddictionaries.com/.

like a desert that is hot in the day but cold in the night. Just as the California desert was transformed into a rich soil, where many fruit trees and vegetables grow, we can and must cultivate this society to be a truly loving and caring place to live.[46]

Lee calls Asian Americans "pioneers," a synonym for pilgrims, who have arrived in the new land. In their hearts, they carry the promise of a just society and caring community. Lee acknowledges this promise is as realistic and vivid as the California desert being transformed into rich soil. As promised in the Abrahamic pilgrim faith, the new land is being transformed into the Promised Land thanks to new Asian (and other ethnic) pilgrims.

What is also unmistakable in the Asian American pilgrim's homiletic of promise is the prominence of the metaphoric concept of land/Land. Land carries a multiplicity of meanings in Asian American life and theology. To begin with, Asian Americans recall their lands being exploited then and now by colonial powers back in Asia. In this sense, land is a reminder of their vulnerability and sorrow. Then, Asian Americans remember the day when they had to leave their thousand-year-old ancestral lands for various reasons—political, economic, legal, etc. In this sense, land is a reminder of their displacement. Further, Asian Americans daily face the fact that they have no lands here in America they can call their own. Of course, they can purchase apartments, buildings, or ranches, yet they are still considered "strangers" and "aliens" in their communities. In this sense, land is a reminder of their temporary stay and status that inevitably burdens their psychology every day. Therefore, it is no wonder that the pilgrim preacher's message of the Promised Land is so desirable and powerful for Asian Americans. The preacher's message promises the eschatological *Third Land* existing beyond Asian lands to which the people cannot go back and beyond American lands to which they cannot truly belong. What's more, the preacher's message acknowledges that this *Third Land* is not only eschatological, but also can become a reality even in this new land; that is, such preaching envisages hostile American lands being transformed into the Promised Land or the postcolonial Third Space of *perichoresis*, as Sarah Travis would say.[47] The pilgrim preacher calls all Asian Americans to

---

46. Lee's sermon, "Our Thanksgiving Day," (unpublished) quoted in his book, *Korean Preaching*, 119.

47. Relying on the Moltmannian-Trinitarian concept of *perichoresis*, Sarah Travis is convinced that postcolonial preaching creates the liberative and reconciliatory perichoretic space in the midst of the exclusive, oppressing colonial social milieu. According to Moltmann, *perichoresis* is "a movement from one to another to reach round and go around, to surround, embrace, and encompass." The Persons of the Trinity within and through this cooperative and mutual inner movement creates spaces for one another's different existence and move in perfect harmony. Travis proposes the social-Trinitarian

be active agents of this grand promise of God. They *are* indeed already agents of transformation because from the very beginning Asians have been called to the promise of the Promised Land just like Abraham and Sarah were. The preacher's important task is to remind the people of this sacred calling, which serves as their core self-identity in the new land—namely, that of the transformative pilgrim.

Finally, as explicitly indicated along the way, the Asian American preacher of the promise (of the Promised Land) carries in and out of herself the homiletic image of the *fellow pilgrim*. The typical images of the preacher as herald, pastor, poet/storyteller, and witness[48] do not seem to do full justice to the homiletic-spiritual nature of the Asian American preacher. The conventional four images of the preacher are all good at describing specific characteristics of the individual preacher, depending on the preacher's own personality or spiritual formation. But they do not have enough concern for the preacher's particular socio-ecclesial context, the place and community out of which the preacher arises. Given the foundational theological ethos of pilgrimage in Asian American ecclesia, no image delineates the Asian American preacher as well as does that of pilgrim.

Why then an emphatic addition of *fellow*—thus, *fellow pilgrim*? Because the main sermonic staple of the Asian American preacher is *collective stories* and the *communal witness* of God's ongoing revelatory events within the community. The Asian American preacher is the one who shares the communal stories of the God-called pilgrims, experienced together on the shared pilgrim journey in the same wilderness. The preacher's genuine authority does not rely on her own private or esoteric experience of God's revelation, but primarily

---

application of *perichoresis* in postcolonial preaching that will eventually help transform the colonial social space of exclusivity and hostility into the boundless space of mutual inclusivity and hospitality. This perichoretic-Trinitarian thought of the harmonious social space finds a great affinity with the Asian American postcolonial yearning for the Promised Land or the Third Land. Travis, *Decolonizing Preaching*, 60–63; Moltmann, *Experiences in Theology*, 156.

48. Long, *The Witness of Preaching*, 19–51. Briefly defined, *the herald* (or *the prophet*) is the authority figure who receives directly from God and brings down straight to the people the very Word of God, while *the pastor* is the one whose pastoral concerns over the people's needs shapes the content of the sermon. *The storyteller/poet* is the preacher whose personal artistic or aesthetic telling of the biblical story stirs the people's hearts and minds to an existential, revelatory experience. *The witness* seems to be the closet one to *the fellow pilgrim* in the sense that the witness also develops intimate ecclesiastical relationship with "the place and community out of which the preacher arises." Yet, the witness shows a significant difference (from the fellow pilgrim) with his/her primary focus on sharing/preaching their own experiential testimony (what is seen and heard uniquely) about God's Word and revelatory events.

on her heart-felt participation in the common people's everyday struggles of pilgrimage. Thus, Kim preaches:

> My husband and I were in awe like the Israelites who were amazed when they first saw the manna in the wilderness, the layer of white flaky substance, covering the ground in great abundance. The manna from heaven, the divine gift! . . . Feeling the divine presence through the snow, I whispered to God "Thank you! Thank you, Lord! You are with us even in this wilderness [of America]!"[49]

In this sermon, the preacher appears as a fellow pilgrim who knows exactly what it means and how it feels to live as a stranger in the wilderness and also who knows exactly how to interpret it from a pilgrim's perspective. The preacher shares the same joy, agony, hopes, and prayers with her own people who are on the same pilgrim journey. The only difference is her unique role as the preacher, a trumpeter who is to proclaim the good news or the promise of God on behalf of all the other fellow pilgrims. In the sermon, the preacher and her fellow pilgrims have begun to taste the fruits the Promised Land of God already accomplished—the Grand Promise they have kept in their hearts since their faithful departure from Asia to the present day. And it is the same Promise they will carry into the future for the next generations of pilgrims from all ethnic groups.

CONCLUSION

Asian Americans, having been uprooted from their original lands and living in a hostile foreign land, have developed triple consciousness as a socio-ecclesial coping mechanism, adding the third identifier of Christian pilgrim to their dual social identities of Asian and American. What essentially goes in tandem with the pilgrim identity is the promise of the Promised Land. This is not a tautology at all because Asian Americans believe that by the same call to be pilgrims they have inherited the Abrahamic promise, the original Promised Land faith, as their own promise. The Abrahamic promise has become their own promise issuing from the same God and the same call.

Above, I showed how the pilgrim preacher developed a homiletic of promise based on this pilgrim theology and spirituality of the Promised Land. At the core of such preachers' sermonic message is the synthetic establishment of the Promised Land as being both this-earthly and other-worldly. Moving a step further from Augustine, Asian Americans have placed an equal emphasis on both, the former hostile foreign land being transformed into

49. Kim, *Preaching in an Age of Globalization*, 126.

the latter as *promised* yet with an eschatological prospect. This is why their preaching is *proclamation* of promise, and not *pronouncement* of promise.[50] They preach something that is actively happening and will happen more in a great expectation.

If I were to end this essay right now, I might rightly be cautioned that the promise of the Promised Land ought not to be exploited by Asian Americans for their own sake alone. The same promise and its projected goals should be extended to all fellow pilgrims from all other racial-ethnic groups. Noting the caution, Kim again provides an insightful antidote in her sermon mentioned above:

> We're pilgrims called by God
> to continue struggling
> until the day when all immigrant people,
> not only [Asians] but also other ethnic groups [are welcomed].

The promise of God is for all, that is, all Whites, Blacks, Browns, Reds, etc., journeying together on and beyond the American soil as the shadow of the Ultimate Promised Land. Yet, Asian Americans know this shadow is as real as the Ultimate one. The Ultimate Promised Land is already here, joyfully proclaimed!

---

50. According to the dictionary, proclamation denotes saying things that are happening now or will happen by someone's action or active involvement, while pronouncement refers to things that have already happened or are already determined to exist in certain ways. In short, proclamation is more present- and future-oriented whereas pronouncement more past- and present-oriented. See the terms "proclamation" and "pronouncement" at http://www.oxforddictionaries.com/.

2

A Promising, Trivocal Hermeneutic for Twenty-First-Century Preaching

Justice, Transformation, and Hope

—Kenyatta R. Gilbert

Preaching is the principal mode by which Christianity has and continues to speak to the ultimate concerns of humankind. In North America and in various parts of the world, humanity has entered a new global reality marked by radical pluralism with all of its complexity. The postmodern challenge of Christian theology is to achieve the status of "global theology," which is reached through contextual theologies that unify the theological enterprise and allow it to speak to the particularities of diverse contexts and extend to the concerns and contexts of a global environment. The two very big issues touched on in this essay are 1) the fragmentation of homiletical curriculum as theological resource for preaching (how do we recover a sense of holism in the curriculum) and 2) the challenge of global homiletical theology (how does Christian preaching today speak to a pluralist world and how do our contextualized homiletical theologies speak to larger concerns beyond their immediate contexts).

African American preaching, reconceived *trivocally*, leads us to a global homiletic theology and thus towards something well beyond the contexts from which it emerges. But what methodological framework could be brought to bear to answer questions such as: *What hermeneutic should govern the course* of African American preaching today? How might African American preaching as a distinctive discourse be shaped to embody more fully the normative purposes of the Christian faith and urge all justice and hope seekers, irrespective of race, ethnicity, or subcommunity, toward a unified vision of "beloved community"? And what does it mean to declare homiletically that Jesus has shown up in our preaching for the good of the community? Answering these questions exhaustively is impossible. But thinking about them critically in terms of interconnections, relationships, and systems, giving attention to the interactive dynamics of the spoken Word, circumstances, and contexts from which and to which words are spoken (i.e., through the lens of practical theology for homiletical instruction), enables preachers to reclaim a more robust homiletical theology for their contexts and speak to larger concerns beyond their immediate contexts as proclaimers of the gospel today.[1]

One way to think about trivocal, proclamatory holism theologically is to relate the ministry of preaching to a vision of Christian eschatology—a perspective on divine intentionality and promise—relative to the past, present, and future. In the context of Hebrew scripture, eschatology is connected to the cultic life of Israel and Israel's messianic expectation of a divine warrior defeating their foreign foes. But also, in contradistinction, eschatology, more broadly, is viewed and interpreted in relation to Jesus' understanding of his mission and message and his resurrection. A rejection of Israel's nationalistic, parochial view of salvation and apocalyptic expectation,[2] the history of promise, as interpreted and codified by the New Testament authors, finds fulfillment in the person and work of Jesus Christ. Thus, as Hans Schwarz puts it, "no promise remains outstanding in the New Testament."[3] If this is so, then to preach the gospel of Jesus Christ is no less than speaking of a promise-bearing God who addresses the real needs of real people.

Our need for contemporary preachers to obtain a fully formed homiletical theology could not be more urgent. In our age of intense political, religious, and social upheaval, preachers must become more self-aware about why today they must more explicitly convey in their sermons, and in their actions that stem from them, a preaching life that is earnest and authentically Christian. A trivocal hermeneutic provides an investigative framework for contemporary preachers to think theologically and introspectively about preaching as an expression of holistic Christian proclamation, and how such proclamation bears a promissory message of hope in a deathly world. For in preaching, the hope of God speaks. The question posed and addressed in this essay is: *How might*

1. Osmer, *Practical Theology*, 17.
2. Schwarz, "Eschatology," 157.
3. Ibid.

the use of the scriptural images of prophet, priest, and sage and the basic tenets of three models of interdisciplinary work in practical theology furnish an intellectually robust, holistic, and constructive theological hermeneutic for contemporary preaching? Drawing on three contemporary models of interdisciplinary work widely recognized in the field of practical theology in dialogue with the central concerns of African American theology reveals how a constructive synchronization of these interdisciplinary models and reconsideration of their basic tenets offer a promising hermeneutical strategy for improving twenty-first-century preaching.

A veritable hermeneutic for Christian preaching must take seriously the theological, biblical, sociopolitical, and pastoral interactive dynamics of the spoken Word, and the listening communities in which and to which the saving message of the gospel is shared and interpreted. The conceptual matrix for understanding the trivocal hermeneutic I am proposing attends to the issue of what I believe to be the most important tasks of the preacher: interpreting scripture and demonstrating how one's method of interpretation and sociocultural context inform the preacher's operative theology (the preacher's individual take on the Christian tradition) in the preaching task. The holistic impulse of the trivocal hermeneutic is perhaps its most notable feature because its fundamental aim is to beckon postmodern preachers to preach the whole counsel of Scripture, proclaiming the promises of God in light of the principles of divine justice, spiritual transformation, and realistic hope. Holistic preaching has a "global" outlook because it proclaims a fully-present Christ in community as access to salvation for all Christian communities—a Christ whose life, revealed by the Spirit, inspires a community's work, unites its members in love, and points the local fellowship of believers beyond its intra-community strivings to an ideal communion of all the saints—a "beloved community." The term "beloved community" has taken on a usage that neglects several rich meanings pointed out by American philosopher Josiah Royce, who first coined the term. In his work *The Problem of Christianity*, Royce defines Christianity as a "religion of loyalty" to community. Beloved community is "beloved" because of the "loyalty" (i.e., love, devotion, and sacrifice) expressed for its establishment and continuation. Royce used the term "beloved community" as a synonym for and better descriptor of the Christian idea and ideal of "kingdom of God" which is the conception of "universal community." According to Royce, essential to social groups achieving the status of community is their having a process (or processes) for interpretation (hermeneutic) for building relationship. Unfortunately, some contemporary theologians think of global theology with regard to achieving consensus or agreement around doctrine and possibly certain liturgical (sacramental) and moral practices. Based on Royce's theory, global theology would be a framework for fostering and furthering dialogue and cooperation that enriches community (just community) on which all humans depend for survival and human fulfillment.[4] Critical reflection on the triadic dynamic outlined in the sections to follow demonstrates how a theoretically reconceived view of African American preaching, drawing on three models of interdisciplinary work in practical theology, furnishes teachers of preachers an intellectually robust and constructive theological hermeneutic for guiding contemporary preaching into a promising future, as it strives to meet the challenges of a new global reality.

CONTEXT-SENSITIVE PEDAGOGY MATTERS: LOCATION, INVASION, AND TRANSGRESSION

Preachers construct identity and encode experience in living communities. Whether the preacher comes to her or his community carrying pre-modern views about the validity of the Bible and Christian doctrine or filters his or her religious experience in deference to the empirical gods of science and logic, peeling away the husks of credulity to appease the modern mind, or ushers in deconstructive tools to decenter modernism's reliance on empirical formulae, scrutinizing the data to see if its theological posture honors inclusivity, pluralism, and diversity, the preacher's words never escape the social contexts which shape them. Despite David Randolph's 1998 proposal, *Renewal of 21st Century Preaching*, which appropriated Ebeling's *new* Hermeneutic as a decentering counter-proposition to Broadus' theologically disengaged *old* rhetoric-driven *On the Preparation of the Delivery of the Sermon* (1870) and birthed a revolution in North American homiletics, homiletic proposals have in general uncritically accepted many Enlightenment presuppositions and their enduring consequences. Few contemporary proposals have emerged that are purposely designed to speak to a religiously fragmented pluralist world. Most have tended toward foundationalist assumptions for preaching. This has had detrimental effects for preaching birthed in socially marginalized communities.

But even if it would be inaccurate to suggest that African American preachers have completely yielded homiletical agency to biblical and theological commentators external to their lived reality and ultimate concerns, it is not wide of the mark to claim that a stubborn strand of anti-intellectualism

---

4. Royce, *The Problem of Christianity*, 41, 44–45, 76, 125, 133, 194, 206, 318, 356, 402–5.

and false intellectualism born of a hermeneutic of misplaced trust in African American preaching, persists, refusing to die the death it needs to die. Therefore, the tradition's capacity to overcome typecasting and caricature remains an enduring problem. Based on the quantity of sermons I have heard preached by African American preachers throughout my teaching career and based on research findings from a congregational study[5] in which I participated, aside from performative revisions, the religious scaffolding of parrot theology in Black religious practices still outpaces an openness to culturally indigenous hermeneutical approaches. This is a theological tragedy as the twenty-first century unfolds since the principal mode by which Christianity has and continues to speak to the ultimate concerns of humankind is through the spoken Word.

The focus of my work in homiletics is intentionally context-specific, and at the same time my teleological aims are intentionally transgressive in terms of thinking about finding ways to invite all human beings to name their own storied realities and common share in the larger society. In a practical sense, however, Asian/Asian Americans, Latinos/as, and womanists, for example, might find resemblances of their own homiletical consciousness in the narrative I construct. But because identity construction, geographical place, and perceptions of hope (as discussed later) can mean different things from one community to another, we do well to tell our own stories. This is not to negate the importance of fostering ecumenicity and Christian unity, but rather is an expansive view to the end of helping individuals see themselves as communally shaped beings having a share as co-participants with God in bringing about a just society where all persons are viewed as having equal worth in God's economy. So, as an African American theorist, I come to my work at best suspicious and at worst alarmed when scholars refuse to acknowledge theological blindspots or scrutinize pedagogical practices and ethnocentric biases. Hermeneutical strategies for preaching that fail to admit that theological points of view are privileged or disregarded based on social location are intellectually dishonest and ultimately will not hold up its end of the deal in a context of religious threat and theological insecurity.

The coming together of Euro-American homiletician Sally Brown and African American homiletician Luke Powery, Reformed-tradition-shaped and Baptist-Wesleyan/Pentecostal-formed respectively, in their co-authored book *Ways of the Word: Learning to Preaching for your Time and Place* (2016), marks a refreshing deviation from the current catalogue of introductory preaching texts. They have offered the discipline a volume honoring the community-forming work of the Spirit. Urging readers toward a Spirit-driven

---

5. Gilbert and Mingo, "The Preached Word," 9–23.

theology for preaching, Brown and Powery have propitiously anticipated the pedagogical challenge of "global theology." Such a contribution is significant given the current picture of homiletics because clergy leaders are still being trained to think and preach from an outflow of circumscribed ideals that follow theoretical principles and guidelines, techniques, and approaches that are either supposedly historically and culturally neutral or privilege views of a certain theological family to the disregard of others. Whether religiously conservative, moderate, or liberal in orientation, theological seminaries and divinity schools often become principal players in domesticating the student preacher's voice. As a child of the South who migrated northeast for seminary, I know the domestication process firsthand. Having attended a predominately Euro-American seminary where Reformed theological points of view are privileged, I quickly learned that doing well in preaching class carried with it the expectation that I would cope with and conform to a particular set of homiletical norms without having space to question their presuppositions or authority.

My criticism here has less to do with the seminarian's need for theological stretching but rather more to do with resisting racializing pedagogy that disciplines learners to see the world through European eyes, thus establishing Whites as global tutors. If homiletics instructors have not frequently visited or preached in ecclesial contexts dissimilar from their own, then they have restricted their homiletical vision and moral authority to share wisdom. Because persons of color early on are taught to read life racially, that is, to define oneself culturally and racially against unrelenting patterns of comparisons and false perceptions of White privilege birthed in colonialism, as theologian Willie Jennings avers, preachers of color have to be especially vigilant and theologically alert to the ways socially dominant and culturally privileged Westernized communities inject imperialism, commodify cultural work, and bound "blackness and the production of its aesthetic values to the schemes and performances of whiteness."[6] Recognizing this aesthetic struggle as a cultural predicament is important. To have a clear understanding of the theological challenge of seeing Jesus rightly as one who renders individuals capable of reframing their own visual ecology to see themselves as God's beautiful ones in a socially fragmented age is crucial for preachers. If the preacher does not name the racial aesthetic regime in theological practice a theological failure, then the people who listen to that preacher will have a malformed picture of their right to human dignity and God-confirmed identity.[7]

---

6. Jennings, "The Aesthetic Struggle and Ecclesial Vision," 163–64.

7. Ibid., 184–85.

Nowhere is the devaluing and disruption of peoplehood in culturally-determined ecosystems more evident than in the production, wide distribution, and heedless consumption of evangelism materials and methods used to indoctrinate and catechize members of culturally marginalized and socially disempowered groups. The early missionary movements in the colonies such as the Church of England's Society for the Propagation of the Gospel to the Heathen in the Foreign Parts (1701) sought to convert Africans without altering the African slave's social position. As indicated in the "discipling for Christ" homiletical methods and conversion strategies of American Evangelicals and Protestant mainliners' mission movements in underdeveloped countries, proselytizing campaigns have primarily focused on "soul-winning" absent providing practical tools for equipping converts to be justice fighters against human exploitation in their contexts. Global evangelism without prophetic core commitments is gospel deficient and more socially regressive than politically liberative.

African American theology, when expressly Christian, "represents an understanding of God's freedom and the good news of God's call for all humankind to enter life in genuine community, with true human identity and moral responsibility."[8] Christian beliefs and practices declared normative today, though taken for granted, do not take rise out of thin air but are culturally-conditioned. The Christian religious movements that have become mainstream in American society trace their heritage from Western theocultural beliefs and practices that are historically conditioned. The sixteenth-century Protestant Reformation began in Europe not in Africa. The reason this is not insignificant is because the brand of Christianity introduced to enslaved Africans assumed a void in the theological and moral content of West African religious traditions and ontological systems. All theology is local. A sensitiveness to the experimental quality and profound symbols of the African's sacred cosmology was never figured into the works of Martin Luther, John Calvin, and Huldrych Zwingli or the theological concepts popularized by their pre-Reformation Roman Catholic forebears, Thomas a Kempis, John Wycliffe, and Peter Waldo. In the same way the cultural provenance of foundational

---

8. According to Ware one can only come to an apt description of African American theology if one understands that human fulfillment and the freedom to flourish are the deep symbols and central concerns of African American theology. African American theology, as Ware defines it, "is a study and interpretation of religious beliefs and practices regarded by African Americans as significant, having either positive or negative consequences for their existence and quality of life." It is shaped and can be explained in terms of four phenomena: 1) the resistance to discrimination and oppression; 2) the body-soul problem (separation into either a soulless body or bodiless soul); 3) religious humanism; and 4) black ethnic identity/racial consciousness. *African American* Theology, 24–25.

Christian thinkers such as Augustine of Hippo, Origin, and Athanasius of the early church shaped their theological question sets and influenced their theological visions, they also shaped the sacred imaginings of continental theologians Karl Barth and Paul Tillich in the post-World War milieu. As tradition-bearing individuals constructing identity in communities reading and interpreting scripture to address life's ultimate concerns, we who preach the gospel must acknowledge that with God on whose behalf we speak, "there is a double relativity: our interpretations are relative to (conditioned by) the presuppositions we bring with us, and those presuppositions, as humans, all too human, are themselves relative (penultimate, revisable, even replaceable) and not absolute."[9]

This is why one's perspective on eschatology is crucial. According to philosophical theologian Frederick Ware the development of conceptions, articulation of ideas, and critique of ideas about human destiny for African American theologians center on eschatology. Whether these conceptions conjure visions of a "glorious black past," "the American dream," "beloved community," the "millennium" or "the second coming of Jesus Christ,'" these concepts, claims Ware, function to offer Black people hope—a way of thinking about their world and the world to come, not as utopian fiction but as a divine promise made in the present and enacted in both the present and future on their behalf.[10] As evident in the spirituals, enslaved Africans, guided by conscience and desire for freedom, fashioned a biblical hermeneutic derived from literal and figurative interpretations of texts surrounding Christ's return and establishment of God's kingdom on earth. Since the Bible, hope, moral behavior, and history are key theological sources for Black Christians and because the "kingdom of God is goal and norm . . . Black eschatology is suspicious of the arrogance and triumphalism of American millennialism."[11] For

---

9. Westphal, *Whose Community? Which Interpretation?*, 15.

10. Ware, *African American Theology*, 172.

11. Related to American civic life, as Ware describes it, the term "millennialism," refers to religious and political perspectives about history's end coupled with an optimistic view of a promising future. In Christian thought, millennialism is divided into three perspectives. Holding a distinctly American view first introduced by Puritans in the colonial period, *postmillenialists* believe Jesus will return after a literal thousand-year reign of peace and prosperity. Second, having roots in Augustinian tradition and remaining the dominant Christian eschatological perspective in Christian denominations today, *amillenialists*, see the thousand-years symbolically, representing the current church, which Jesus will reclaim upon his return. Finally, broken into two branches—*classical* or *nondispensationalists* and *dispensationalists*—*premillenialists* view world deterioration as the sign of the end and not progress or improvement. Premillenialists put little stock in redeeming a world they believe is doomed for destruction and therefore claim that the church's mission should primarily focus on evangelism—"saving souls." Although each of

this reason, and to esteem past experiences, African Americans created their own Black millennialism, which affirmed the notion that the prudent use of what American culture has to offer and working within its social institutions could have socially transformative effect; that American society and Western civilization stands to face divine judgment for its sins; and that initiating a new age of equality, justice, and peace will be the church's chief work and responsibility.[12]

Because the Christian religion has thrived largely through cultural myth-making and from political battles fought in closed quarters, the global challenge today is not to get all Christian communities to sit under the same canopy of religious experience by universalizing or socializing [individuals] to a white gold standard, rather the twenty-first century challenge is to call communities established in Christ's name to name and conscientiously embrace their equal share in Jesus' holy and beloved vision of communal care and moral and ethical responsibility.

IS AN APT DESCRIPTION OF AFRICAN AMERICAN PREACHING OBTAINABLE?

African American preaching is aesthetically rich discourse with emancipatory ends. It is foremost an act of worship—spoken and embodied Word that inspires faith in Jesus Christ. Preaching of this kind uses the power of language and art to interpret the gospel—on God's behalf, in service to the gospel of Jesus Christ for the community. When I use the term African American "trivocal preaching," I am referring to preaching primarily marked by distinctive, interrelated accents—a three-dimensional dynamic—at work within the tradition when brought into its proper focus (although, in many veiled or unfocused ways, a particular dimension or voice is often privileged over or used in disregard of the other). Accordingly, a *trivocal hermeneutic* is a constructive interpretive strategy for doing theology holistically for the pulpit, and for meeting the challenge of Christian theology to achieve the status of global theology. Three scriptural accents describe the hermeneutic. To summarize, the *prophetic* voice mediates God's activity to transform church and society in a present-future sense based on the principle of justice. The *priestly*

---

these forms of Christian millennialism might be present in African American congregations, Black liberation theologians have reworked conceptions of Christian millennialism to distinctively create their own Black millennialism. Cf. F. Ware, "On the Compatibility/Incompatibility of Pentecostal Premillenialism with Black Liberation Theology," 191–92; Ware, *African American Theology*, 175–176.

12. Ware, *African American Theology*, 179.

voice attends to the Christian spiritual formation and transformation of hearers by encouraging them to contemplate their personal relationship with their Creator and enhance themselves morally and ethically. The *sagely* voice carries a sapient function and is distinguished by its focus on the preacher's and congregation's wisdom, treasured past, and realistic hope for future generations.

Based on the community-transforming details surrounding Jesus' inaugural vision recorded in Luke 4: 16–21, the trivocal method of interpretation derives from seven particulars of Jesus' norm-setting vision for Christian proclamation. In his reading the scroll of Isaiah's messianic prediction, Jesus' offers a vision for ministry that 1) is sociopolitical in character; 2) invites human participation; 3) rallies a community to accept their religious obligation to serve God by expressing God's concern for community wellness; 4) reiterates the fact that life in the context of community is less than perfect; 5) calls into question social arrangements that exploit the poor and religious rituals that baptize the status quo; 6) points to the fact that community wellness is a divine concern; and 7) acknowledges that the vision is not fully realized. I define *trivocally conscious preaching* (African American preaching):

> as a ministry of Christian proclamation—a theo-rhetorical discourse about God's good will toward community with regard to divine intentionality, communal care, and the active practice of hope—that find resources internal to Black life [or perhaps any circumscribed justice and hope seeking subcommunity homologously established] in the North American context.[13]

Trivocally conscious preaching is catalytic and holistic when this three-dimensional dynamic is at work within the tradition, functioning with mutually critical influence in a counterbalancing relationship. When these voices are synthesized and appropriated in one's preaching, they establish for the preacher an operational framework for measuring the depth and reach of the preacher's homiletical offering. This working definition provides us a handle for examining the operational theology in play as the preacher responds to the broad range of complex congregational and secular community concerns and expectations, in light of the preacher's interaction with the scriptures and the principal requirements of Jesus' norm-setting inaugural vision as clearly outlined in Luke 4:16–21.

---

13. Gilbert, *Journey and Promise*, 11.

Toward a Homiletical Theology of Promise

THE TRIVOCAL IMPULSE: A CALL TO HOLISTIC PREACHING

African American Prophetic Preaching

The common thread of all prophetic preaching traces from the recognition of injustice, and that the preacher will name injustice for what it is, and what justice should be.[14] Prophetic preaching is "interpretation" that brings clarity to the sacred (God, revealed truth, highest moral values, etc.) and articulates what should be appropriate human response to the sacred. The preacher who preaches prophetically does not treat social justice (or other sacred values) as something independent from God but rooted in and emanating from God. Prophetic preaching is mediational in a present-future sense, and fundamentally, a rhetoric of humanization—a sacred discourse about divine intentionality. It is spoken Word that begins in supplication and attends to human tragedy to hear God's revelation, and its procedure for broadcasting what is received to the human audience for whom it is intended.[15] Prophetic preaching is neither imported nor self-generated witness, but is mediated and worked out in community, not in isolation.

Jeremiah, the Hebrew *nabi'* (most often translated as prophet), meaning "one who is called" or "one who calls forth" is paradigmatic in that he receives an appointment from God to a work of "building up, and tearing down" (Jer 1:10). Jeremiah, Elijah, Jonah, Moses, and Ezekiel, were often called into communities who resisted their speech and opposed their work. Jeremiah's "Temple sermon" (7:1–15) is an example of this. Believing the Temple and its ritual practices were tools of social control, Jeremiah pronounces God's indictment upon "shepherds [i.e., the religious leaders and monarchial leadership] who have scattered the sheep" for their evil doings.[16] The prophet is also paradigmatic for seeing prophetic preaching's synthetic impulse. Jeremiah not only proclaims God's judgment on Israel but he acts as a priest to the Hebrew exiles taken into Babylonian captivity. As prophet-priest, Jeremiah is "called to be a child of the tradition, one who has taken it seriously in the shaping of his or her own field of perception."[17] Any examination into the nature and function of prophetic preaching lifts and values the mutually enriching relationship between biblical interpretation and sociocultural contexts.

---

14. Gilbert, *Pursued Justice*, 6.
15. Ibid.
16. Ibid., 57.
17. Brueggemann, *Commentary on Jeremiah*, 78.

More contemporarily, one might observe how the prophetic preaching of a few African American clergy in the urban North responded to community crisis during the out-migration of southern laborers who exited the racially hostile Jim Crow South in droves and flooded their sanctuaries. These northern clerics spoke to social ills created by the war, the rise of industry, and the expansion of ghettos in northern cities. Though not an even exchange in terms of southern victimization and abuse, upon northern resettlement most Black people experienced social death and disillusionment having to contend with job discrimination, unfair hiring practices, neighborhood redlining, and intra-racial crime. The strident sermons of African American clerics such as Junius Caesar Austin, Lacey Kirk Williams, and Florence Spearing Randolph, criticized injustice, paired hope with circumstance, and addressed specific congregational and community-wide corporate concerns.

African American prophetic preaching is a rhetoric of humanization that is not fundamentally different from prophetic preaching in general, except to the extent that is seen as God-summoned speech clothed in cultural particularity.[18]

African American Priestly Preaching

As spoken Word, operationally, priestly preaching is sacramental mediation. This dimension of African American preaching emphasizes Christian spiritual formation and the importance of congregational worship and being justified, redeemed, and sanctified by Jesus' atoning works. But not only this, in keeping with reminding hearers of God's faithfulness and promise keeping, priestly preaching interprets and mediates the requirements of covenantal obligation to God and God's people. Priestly preaching casts the preacher as prayerful intercessor, congregational care agent, and safeguard of the institutional life of the church. However resplendent the preacher's words are as priest, if ritualistic observances cultivate attitudes of apathetic resignation by neglecting the soul care or spiritual needs of desperately hurting people in the world or is disassociated from Jesus' sending commission to *go and make disciples of all nations, baptizing them in the name of the Father and of the Son and of the Holy Spirit* (Matt 28:13), then that preacher's address fails its principal agenda of becoming a psychic, physical, and spiritual healing resource.

Regrettably, a deep hermeneutical divide persists as many preachers see their work one-dimensionally, through an operational lens exclusively focused on addressing matters of orthodoxy, personal piety, evangelism, and spiritual

---

18. Gilbert, *Pursued Justice*, 6.

formation. Or, by contrast, preachers who criticize liturgical and formative practices when they do not prepare believers to actively engage larger community concerns such as racial profiling, mass incarceration, gender inequity, and educational disparity, and economic injustice can be equally theologically near-sighted. Christian social ethicist Peter Paris best conceives the negative impact on community wellness when the prophetic witness is decoupled from priestly witness. When the prophetic and priestly dialectic are not held together, he contends, all available means to effect religious and moral reform in the public square and aiding and abetting the race in its capacity to endure social dehumanization is effectively cut off.[19]

African American priestly preaching works in the direction of assisting congregations to negotiate faithful possibilities for creatively synthesizing their historical and ritual identities—while consciously reforming and affirming their charter in modern times.[20]

African American Sagely Preaching

African American sagely preaching is wisdom directed and peculiarly communal; as spoken Word, it confers biblical wisdom and realistic hope for future generations as it reflects on the past and present witness of a congregation's story in society. The preacher's homiletical task centers on gathering up the artifacts, relevant concerns, and specific events in a particular congregation's life story and sets them in the larger drama of God's active presence in the world. The preacher's interpretive and proclamatory posture is formed by her or his radical embrace of what Alyce McKenzie describes as a "sapiential hermeneutic"[21]—an interpretive strategy that honors the consecrated preacher and awaiting congregation antiphonal, egalitarian, and mutually enriching relationship. It casts the same title upon both preacher and worshipping community: sage.[22] The sagely dimension of the preacher's witness is consonant with the African *jali's* principal task as poet and repository of the community's oral tradition. In song and storytelling, the *jali* or griot would gather the collective wisdom of the people, reminding them of their historical function as carriers of culture with an obligation to keep alive cultural identity-forming practices for community survival.

---

19. Paris, *Social Teachings of Black Churches*, 11.
20. Gilbert, *Journey and Promise*, 61.
21. McKenzie, "The Company of Sages," 92.
22. McKenzie, *Preaching Biblical Wisdom in a Self-Help Society*, 35.

To the listening congregation, sagely preaching poses questions such as, "Where do we as a community go from here based on who we say we are religiously? And how must we, in community, express our commitment to God through song and symbol in the world?" The preacher as sage is entrusted with the congregation's faith identity. In the act of proclamation the preacher sage reminds believers of their commitments as redeemed persons who have declared allegiance to the crucified and risen sage—Jesus Christ.[23]

A promising hermeneutic for twenty-first-century preaching is trivocal because it gathers up three interpretive strands for seeing the work of the preacher in a theologically robust manner "unifying" (or harmonizing) the scriptural images of prophet, priest, and sage in Christian preaching and seeks to situate African American preaching in a larger context and global reality. Homiletical holism is the goal, the measure, and guiding force for contextually fitting, theologically relevant, and biblically sound Christian preaching in our increasingly pluralistic world of intense social change.

African American sagely preaching enables community constructive intergenerational conversations to take place and helps members to honor their history of communally shared witness while journeying as a congregation trusting in God.

INTERDISCIPLINARY IMPLICATIONS FOR TRIVOCAL PREACHING

Now I want to give focused attention to three contemporary models of practical theology relative to a trivocally conscious hermeneutic, to demonstrate how a reconsideration of their basic tenets mutually enriches the other, and how, when drawn into creative dialogue, enable a constructive way of reconceiving preaching more holistically. The first model to be discussed is the *revised praxis correlational model*. Correlationalists have asserted that practical theology is genuinely constructive when theology and other disciplines are brought into mutually influential dialogue. The revised correlational model is an offshoot of Paul Tillich's theological method of correlation. Tillich argued that theology answers questions raised by culture when the arts and sciences enter into dialogue. According to Tillich's view of the history of Christian thought, theologians and churches to which they belong have always "correlated" (related) their faith with the challenges and questions raised in their period of history. But more recently scholars such as David Tracy and Don Browning have proposed the *revised correlational model*, having suggested

---

23. McKenzie, *Preaching Proverbs*, xxi.

that Tillich's theological method is inadequate based on the view that theology and the arts and sciences should function on equal plane. Tracy and Browning ask: Why should theology have privilege over the human sciences? Still, Matthew Lamb and Rebecca Chopp further extend the correlational scheme with a revised praxis model, where the goals of social transformation are essential to forging a mutually influential, cross-disciplinary conversation between theology and the human sciences.[24]

A second model, like the correlationalists', is the *transformational model*, which was first proposed by the late James E. Loder. Loder claimed that practical theology is constructively used when theology and the human sciences dialogue with one another. However, Loder's *transformational model* differs from those of the correlationalists in its assertion that practical theology is only true to its core principles when theology takes a leading role, which is to say that theology is in the driver's seat and has at least marginal priority over the human sciences in cross-disciplinary conversation.[25] Dale Andrews' *Black Church praxis-covenant model* represents an important opening in practical theology because of its full-bodied appreciation for the theological and ecclesial dynamics so central to African American theology and Christian practice in general and African American preaching in specific. Andrews interprets the estrangement of Black theology from early and contemporary modes of African American folk religion. In contrast to earlier theoretical proposals preoccupied with criticism of White theological normativity, Andrews's work represents the first proposal in Black homiletics that cannot be described as scholarship so highly contextualized that it lacks the capacity to be genuinely constructive for the Christian tradition.

COMBATING DEHUMANIZATION

Critical social theorist Matthew Lamb advocates fostering a mutually influential conversation between new social liberation movements and the Christian community—a conversation focused upon the praxis of each partner. Such praxis, broadly defined, is "the struggle against some concrete form of oppression and includes theoretical reflection that guides this struggle."[26] Lamb claims that interdisciplinary reflection develops from the legitimate questions critical social theorists ask of theologies and ideologies. In view of this notion, Lamb makes two important claims. He first claims that "the scandal of the

---

24. Gilbert, *Journey and Promise*, 64.
25. Ibid.
26. Lamb, *Solidarity with Victims*, 1.

Cross is the scandal of God identified with all the victims of history in the passion of Christ;" therefore, accordingly, "the cries of the victims are the voice of God (*Vox victimarum vox Dei*)."[27] The critical aspect of Lamb's political theology is *agapic* praxis (the self-transcending love of Jesus, the one whose identification with suffering was not passive but overcoming through the power of resurrection, that breaks spiritual the bonds of the human predicament).

Further, Lamb unites *agapic* praxis with noetic (intellectual) praxis, which states that solidarity with the victims of history cannot be genuine if it trivializes the suffering plight of one's neighbor and its claim on our conscience. Genuine solidarity seeks distance from all histories of sufferings. His second claim is that because of the pervasiveness of bias in society, there remains a religious option for displaying discipleship. That option is to struggle for the realization of justice in history that affirms that humankind is not on its own, and that, fundamentally, humans cannot justify themselves.[28] The African American preacher finds critical insight and social legitimization here. The cost of following Jesus is to be prophetic through orthopraxy informed by orthodoxy. But not only this, self-criticism is essential for preachers to respond justly to the "cries of victims" when interpreting the gospel with regard to justice ideals and the active practicing of hope toward emancipatory ends.[29] Though audacious and sometimes forceful, the prophetic voice is not the voice of pulpit authoritarianism. The prophetic dimension of the trivocal hermeneutic undermines pulpit authoritarianism or what Lamb refers to as *sacralism*. When preachers lose sight of Jesus' trivocal vision, preachers will protect their own self-interest rather than the interest of the victims.

Lamb's attention to praxis supports the critical recovery of the prophetic voice in religious practice, however, his program stops short. On the one hand, he narrowly conceives of God's voice as merely the cries of victims. Clearly this is not the only image of God to be derived from Scripture. On the other, he does not seek a broad enough institutional base for his "new way of doing theology," thus its practical and constructive agendas are imbalanced, despite his programs strengths. He collaborates with labor unions, secular racial and ethnic organizations, and White academic theologians to the disregard of enlisting church leaders and seems to overlook the important contributions of pivotal liberation theologians such as James Cone, Jacqueline Grant, and J. Deotis Roberts.

However much one turns to the strength of Lamb's program for developing a robust practical theological framework for holistic preaching, a

27. Gilbert, *Journey and Promise*, 65.
28. Ibid.
29. Ibid.

subsequent question must be asked of his epistemological claims: What comes after liberation? Because we are contingent beings (we cannot free ourselves), in the past, traditional liberationists' response to matters of spiritual oppression and humanity's redemption from corporeal sin against the Creator have been imperceptible and unsatisfactory. For this reason, James E. Loder's transformational model of interdisciplinary work, when held in dialectic tension with Lamb's insights, can give an intrinsic supplement to the prophetic claims of Lamb's model.

THE LOGIC OF THE SPIRIT

Taking his cue from Karl Barth and his interpreters' reading of the divine-human relational dynamic, Loder formulates an approach that presupposes that theology and its non-theological partners stand, conceptually, in an asymmetrical, bipolar relational unity. Loder's scheme is Christological, and his program flows from his interpretation of three aspects of the divine-human relationship. They are *indissoluble differentiation, inseparable unity*, and *indestructible order*.[30] As these aspects suggest, Jesus, the second person of the Trinity, is not simply a human being better than we are, having admirable and holy characteristics and divine attributes, a view championed by pre-WWI liberal theology. Rather, Jesus, in fact, coexists with the Creator and Holy Spirit in a "self-involving" dynamic. The logic of the Spirit, therefore, is seeing Jesus in relation to the other persons of the Trinity in an undifferientiated way. To put it another way, there is no break or disruption of natures in the christological pattern.

For Loder, the divine exercises logical and ontological priority over our creaturely existence. Loder's "interdisciplinary and self-involving" methodology is important in our examination of the African American preacher's functional role as spokesperson of the gospel and community intercessor. A careful examination of his program reveals a priestly element of practical theological reflection that one cannot overlook. The transformational model sheds light on the priestly dimension of the trivocal hermeneutic, which emphasizes the significance of the atoning work of Jesus Christ—the second person of the Trinity. Loder's program provides a way of discussing the sacramental mediation of Christ in preaching, namely, why the believer's status as justified, redeemed, and sanctified heir of God is so deeply connected to the transformative power of the spoken Word and the believer's hope.

---

30. Ibid., 67.

In Loder's schema, transformation has five core dimensions: historical, systematic, ecclesial, operational, and contextual.[31] In his program, the systematic dimension is accorded methodological priority. Systematically, Jesus Christ as described in the Chalcedonian formulation (that Jesus coexists with the Creator and Holy Spirit in a self-involving dynamic) is his starting point. The crucial systematic task is "to point to the mystery of God's nature and action, organizing the human action disciplines in constructive relationship with theological disciplines."[32] Loder's transformational model, in contradistinction to Lamb's revised praxis model, claims that the baseline of a viable practical theology must be theological (theocentric), not experiential (anthropocentric), for if it is experience based, "the relationality may implicitly legitimate incoherence since it overtly rejects universals and affirms justice and narratives as universally applicable."[33]

When carefully considered, the transformational model is useful because it can be compass-setting, reminding the preacher that in order to be faithful to the communal care agenda of Jesus' inaugural vision, the preacher's own spiritual grounding is of crucial importance. As community intercessor and institutional guardian, the preacher's work of calling to worship persons who are gathered in Christ's name carries with it the functional obligation of the preacher setting the tone. In a word, there are no real substitutes for the "ministry of presence." Christ walked among the people, touching, healing, and raising them.

But Loder's model is not without its shortcomings for doing global theology. Theologically, as a practical model it is contextually lacking. In the antebellum period, the slave preacher recognized the inadequacies of the theologically abstract "theology from above" epistemology that has shaped the sacred imagination of much of Euro-American liturgical practice. Slave preachers gave specific emphasis to a God who comes as Incarnate Word—Emmanuel—God with us.[34] The tragic realities that touched the daily lives of the enslaved inspired them to cry out for divine rescue from a trustworthy savior and friend. Enslaved African converts held in tension both a "theology from above" and a "theology from below," and used this dialectic to construct a distinctive theological imagination. Structurally, the Loderian model is too university based, which corresponds rather closely to Lamb's noetic praxis.[35] The philosophical fount from which Loder imbibes flows from

31. Loder, "Normativity and Context in Practical Theology," 359.
32. Ibid., 361–62.
33. Ibid., 363.
34. Gilbert, *Journey and Promise*, 69.
35. Ibid.

Swiss Reformed, Euro-Germanic streams of theological reflection rather than drawing from the formulations of indigenous theology in particular ecclesial multi-racial and multi-ethnic American communal enclaves. Since the 16th century Reformation, Protestant theologians of the West focused principally on the identification and exposition of *loci* (locations), which are regarded as the basic topics of theology. Frederick Ware notes that the major theologians of European universities "framed by loci supposedly [context-neutral] extrapolated from Scripture or based on incontestable authority" posed certain limits on Christianity as a religion for a particular experience of life instead of viewing Christianity as a religion forming a certain quality of life.[36] Although the loci method is widely embraced and taken for granted in the modern period, the Protestant Reformers' and their successors construal of theology based on systematically configured (loci) proofs it seems aimed at a particular quality of life, which has not resulted in any uniformity in theology. Ware explains,

> There are numerous and varying lists of loci. Not only do the lists contain different loci; lists with similar loci are also arranged differently. Melanchthons's *Loci praeceipui theologici* contains twenty-four loci, which include God, creation, freewill, sin, law, gospel, grace, good works, Scripture . . . the loci used by Gerhard are Scripture, God and Trinity, Christ, church, and ministry. The loci used by John Calvin are God, Christ, salvation, and church . . . Barth . . . revelation, God, creation, reconciliation, and redemption . . .[37]

Our construed theological formulations are not prejudice-free, and for all the great benefits of the loci method, it is not without its limits when thinking about doing theology fittingly, i.e., in ways indigenous to one's particular ecclesial habitat. Given, proximate norms and goals are manifested in *koinonia* (fellowship of the saints) for Loder. In light of Loder's university-based structuralist program of relating theology and science to guide practical theological practice and practitioners, the theological conundrum here becomes one of access. Is Loder's transformational model aptly importable for many rural and urban African American communities of faith who are often disconnected from cutting-edge academic resources? How could these communities effectively construct for themselves a bona fide theology consistent with Loder's transformational scheme?[38]

---

36. Ware, *African American Theology*, 6.
37. Ibid., 7.
38. Gilbert, *Journey and Promise*, 69.

Despite these limitations, the transformational model nevertheless offers the preacher/practical theologian a theologically robust model for conceptualizing the pattern of humanity's once-for-all and ongoing redemption. Regrettably, what remains underdeveloped, I think, is a discussion of how his methodology could be refashioned to embody more fully the normative purpose of the Christian life in particular contexts of experience and arise to achieve the status of "global theology." Lamb's revised praxis approach has merit for providing insight into the nature of the prophetic voice, and Loder's transformational agenda speaks roughly to a more priestly dynamic; however, both programs lack color, that is, context-specific content. Conceptually, we are implicitly encouraged to see and accept a doctrine of God and doctrine of the church with no feet in the world of racial/ethnic pluralism. We are not permitted to hear the prophetic and priestly soundings—the voice of the preacher and people—rehearsing the communal story, calling up the journeys of those exemplars of faith or how the stirring and chanting in the power of the Holy Spirit created frenzy and demonstrated the inexpressible nature of Black religious experience.[39] The church was established by Jesus Christ, a disinherited Jew,[40] who by salvation (bringing human beings into relationship with God and one another) and through spiritual adoption receives repentant sinners into familial relationship as a loving parent would a child. Relationships that are meaningful and lasting originate in places where people own a slice of God's story. Christ's church is a covenant community of gathered persons who by divine intent experience the core qualities of wisdom and faith in particular ways. No practical theological model to date articulates this better than Dale Andrews's *Black church praxis-covenant project*.[41]

REFUGE AND FOLK RELIGION

Dale Andrews develops an ecclesiological practical theology for Black churches. For him, the great gift of the Black church is its operative function of being a *refuge*—a reservoir of communal care, religious formation, and liberating

---

39. Ibid., 70.

40. See J. Kameron Carter's *Race: A Theological Account* (New York: Oxford Press, 2008) for an intriguing accounting of the theological processes of how Christ was abstracted from Jesus' Jewish roots and became, effectively, a "white" racialized figure, and thereby launching modernity's intellectual and social processes that ultimately recast Jesus' Jewish covenantal flesh for Jewish racial flesh. What he unpacks is the discursive path upon which theology embarked to legitimate a "modern racial imaginary" inimical to Afro-Christian faith and thus has thrown postmoderns into a theological crisis that forces one to question the future direction of theology.

41. Gilbert, *Journey and Promise*, 70.

hope. As a way to explore the role of faith claims in Black religious folk traditions, he reconsiders the role of faith claims in Black religious folk traditions, and he reconsiders the meaning of survival in the Black church from slavery to the present day. The question he raises is: Is Black Church synonymous with political passivity and social regression? Andrews argues that the Black church has shouldered the unfair burden of these descriptors, especially due to the criticism of Black theologians. He insists that "black theology's sweeping disparagement of the 'otherworldliness' of black churches indicates a misdiagnosis, which actually exposes a glaring 'missed-diagnosis'—American individualism," and thus has obscured the communal picture of the Black church's role and function in society.[42] In effect, these academics, have 1) irresponsibly launched a liberation platform without the Black church's blessing—that is, they have abandoned the wisdom of the Black church and its sagely voice for the culture, and accordingly, have tied their work to Eurocentric methods and secular Black power agendas; and 2) they have overlooked the vast opportunities to observe how liberation ethics, as described through the refuge paradigm, functions in the life of the church.[43]

Andrews outlines four basic tenets in terms of the social function and particular religious witness (faith identity) of Black church religious practice. These four tenets of faith identity center on: 1) the doctrine of creation and concept of *imago Dei*; 2) the symbolic significance of the exodus narrative; 3) the redemptive nature of the sufferings of Christ and the importance of conversion, serving as guiding norms for a comprehensive model of ecclesiology for Black churches; 4) eschatology and the kingdom of God. A faith identity rooted in the concept of imago Dei insists that humans have responsibility to God and intrinsic worth to God. When appropriating the exodus motif, Israel's liberation saga legitimates God's will toward justice for humanity, and this has long been the strong scriptural motif for Black people's struggle against oppressive forces in this country. A developed faith identity focused on Jesus' sufferings does not suggest that suffering is an end but, rather, is "freedom from, or victory over, the ultimately destructive capacity of suffering or evil itself."[44] And, finally, hope flows from Black eschatology. The fullness of God's salvific action displaces despair, and an anticipated future where liberation and reconciliation of humanity takes place is the highest ideal of this fourth dimension. The sagely dimension of the preacher's trivocal hermeneutic gathers these elements of faith identity and names them hope.

---

42. Andrews, *Practical Theology for Black Churches*, 7.
43. Ibid., 51–56.
44. Ibid., 40–42.

For the African American preacher who would confer the community's wisdom and the wisdom of Scripture and inspire realistic hope for future generations, he or she must be homiletically prepared to preach trivocally from the three voices of prophet, priest, and sage. Hence, Andrews' covenant model of Black ecclesiology yields critical insight into the reawakening and vitalization of the life of the religious community in society. What Andrews' project helps us to see is the vital importance of contextualization—taking culture and cultural change seriously. Though Andrews seeks to cull out a thoroughgoing prophetic practical theology, his ecclesiology, in my view, is an integration of all three dimensions of the trivocal hermeneutic. However, in my judgment it is the sagely oriented dimension that is most pronounced. Set in a biblical, historical, sociocultural framework, this interdisciplinary model is about "community" and the shared work of preacher and community in reclaiming the Black church's communal, kinship identity.

Apart from the obvious advantages of thinking critically about what Black ecclesiology usefully offers Black Christians, the forward-reaching exploration of the state of African American preaching today is less attended to in this work. Andrews does not adequately discuss the widening chasm between contemporary Black congregations and the institutional practices and vision of the best of traditional Black folk religion, and how many Black congregations today are ill equipped and ill prepared to engage meaningfully some of the most complex issues of our times. How will the Black church and Black theology fare in meeting the postmodern challenge? While it is certainly the case that Black theologians must admit their failure to diagnose properly the true nature and actual inner workings of churches that operate and have operated as refuge stations, the Black church today must also confront its own failures to outline its vision for liberation and ministerial praxis for the twenty-first century.[45]

In the end, the dialogical element of the Black church praxis-covenant model provides for what is, in effect, preacher/congregation egalitarianism. The implication, then, is that preaching's wisdom share is always dialogical—the interrelationship between spiritual and historical liberation enriches the other and furnishes the common life of a particular worshiping community's wisdom and hope. One of the gifts of folk religion is the sacred harmonies of "call and response."[46]

---

45. Ibid., 44–45.
46. Gilbert, *Journey and Promise*, 73.

CONCLUDING REFLECTIONS: THE HOMILETICAL UPSHOT

Matthew Lamb's liberationist model stops short of this contextually robust presentation of the sagely dynamics of Black religious life and practice, and James Loder's transformational scheme carefully outlines the divine-human relation but seems to overlook the role of how contextually determined people work out their understanding of the incarnational presence of God in their midst. When Lamb, Loder, and Andrews are read and appropriated dialectically for thinking about African American preaching, creative dialogue can be fostered and African American preachers are provided a constructive paradigm to reconceive preaching more holistically. Taken together, they form a useful threefold cord for exploring synchronically the expressed nature and hermeneutical function of trivocal preaching.[47]

A critical appropriation of the rudiments of each—the revised praxis correlational, the transformational, and the Black church praxis-covenant interdisciplinary models—points the preacher as practical theologian toward a more authentic way of preaching and doing theology contextually. These models value the reflexive and introspective character of theory and the concrete realities of praxis in contemporary religious practice.[48] Hence, an approach to homiletics that emphasizes the prophetic, priestly, and sagely dimensions of Christian preaching is fertile ground for meaningfully addressing the state of health of the church's proclamation in our times, rising to the postmodern global homiletical theology challenge of speaking a message of promise to a pluralistic world, and moving us towards something well beyond the contexts from which it emerges, that is, towards a unified vision of *beloved community* and *koinonia* with our neighbor and our God.

---

47. Ibid., 75.
48. Ibid.

— 3 —

The Spirit-Breathed Body

Divine Presence and Eschatological Promise in Preaching

—Ruthanna B. Hooke

"Who dares, who can, preach, knowing what preaching is?"[1] Karl Barth posed this question, and the question indicates the deep seriousness with which he took preaching, and his understanding of the awesome nature of the preaching task. Barth's sense of the daunting nature of the preaching task, and even (considered from the human standpoint) the impossibility of preaching, is closely linked to his sense of the promise of preaching, which is that preaching is nothing less than the Word of God, spoken through human words. This is truly an astonishing and even unfathomable claim—that God should choose to speak through human beings, that humans in all of their particularity, finitude, and brokenness should be channels for the divine presence and Word. It is amazing to claim that preaching represents an opening, a place for the infinite and the holy to make itself manifest. Of course, many have felt that this claim was far too exalted to make for preaching, and have argued instead that preaching is merely human words about God, not in itself a moment of God's presence and speaking. However, the claim of Barth and others that preaching is something more than this, that it is a privileged event of divine-human encounter, is ultimately a more

---

1. Barth, "The Need and Promise of Christian Preaching," 126.

hopeful position to take about preaching, even if it raises the stakes and makes preaching more daunting than if it is considered simply as human speech. It is a hopeful stance to claim that God really does reveal Godself to us, not only in the sacraments, or in the stuff of our ordinary lives, but in a privileged way in this moment when a human being seeks to speak true words about her interpretation of God's revelation in scripture and in life.

Not only is Barth's position a hopeful one to take, but it corresponds to what many preachers actually feel. Having taught many years' worth of beginning preaching students, I can attest that the fear that they feel about preaching, their sense of the awesomeness of the task, stems not only from its being an event of public speaking on matters of life and death importance to them. Rather, their fear (and also their excitement) comes still more from a sense that in preaching they are engaged not only in a human event of speaking and listening, but that they are presenting themselves and their words to be inhabited, used, opened up by God to becoming God's own presence and Word. It is this sense of preaching as an event in which God is active through a human body and human words—a sense perhaps not fully articulated as such, perhaps only obscurely felt—that is the fundamental theological promise upon which preaching rests.

Homiletical theology seeks to investigate how preaching is an exercise in theological reflection—not merely the application of theology generated elsewhere, but rather itself generative of theological claims. A homiletical theology of promise might explore the ways in which the practices, theories, and contexts of preaching generate theological reflection on God's promise. Such reflections might focus on how God's justice and grace are related, and therefore on the eschatological horizon of preaching and of Christian life. This essay, however, will explore not so much the theologies of promise that preaching generates, as the fundamental theological promise that preaching rests upon, which is the promise of God's presence in preaching. The embodied experience of this fulfilled promise in the event of preaching will be taken as the starting point for generating theological reflection on various aspects of God's promise.

God's fundamental promise, "I am with you always, to the end of the age" (Matt 28:20), is true in all aspects of human life, but the claim of Barth and others is that this presence is particularly powerful, gracious, and effective in preaching. This claim—that preaching is an event in which God speaks through human bodies and words—immediately raises a whole host of questions, all centering around the basic question: how is this possible? How does it happen that God speaks and is present through the finite, fallible human preacher? To answer this fundamental theological question is to engage various *loci* in Christian systematic theology, such as doctrines of revelation, theological anthropology, Christology, and ecclesiology. In this paper, the principal *locus* through which I will explore the question of how preaching is possible, how God keeps God's promise to be present through human words and presence, is that of liturgical theology, and sacramental theology as a subset of liturgical theology.

HOMILETICAL THEOLOGY AND LITURGICAL THEOLOGY

It is appropriate for homiletical theology to enter into conversation with liturgical theology because preaching is fundamentally a liturgical act. From the earliest Christian liturgies, the sermon was considered integral to the liturgy, and the two-fold structure of the Liturgy of the Word and the Liturgy of the Table is attested as early as the time of Justin Martyr. Although there is preaching that takes place outside of liturgy, the primary home of preaching is the corporate worship of the Christian assembly. One of the notable features of the liturgical reform movements of the twentieth century has been a renewed recognition of the essential two-fold structure of the liturgy.[2] While Protestant churches have tended to emphasize the Liturgy of the Word at the expense of the Liturgy of the Table, and Roman Catholics tended toward the reverse emphasis, the twentieth century saw a recognition that from earliest times these two parts of the service were meant to be in balance and serve as a counterpoint to each other. As a result of this recognition, Protestant churches began to reincorporate the Eucharist as central to their worship, while Roman Catholics placed a greater emphasis on the sermon than heretofore. As part of these developments, liturgical theologians began to incorporate theological reflection on the sermon as part of the liturgy, and as having its own distinctive role in the liturgy. Homileticians, however, have tended not to place much emphasis on the relationship of the sermon to the rest of the liturgy, and tend not to theorize the sermon as a liturgical act.[3] Homiletical reflection on the sermon as an event tends to view it as standing alone, having its meaning in relationship to Scripture or to the congregation, but not to the event of worship.

There are several benefits to placing homiletics theology in conversation with liturgical theology. First, liturgical theology is fundamentally akin

---

2. Lathrop emphasizes this two-fold structure. See Lathrop, *Holy Things*, 43–53.

3. Notable exceptions include Rice, *The Embodied Word* and Greenhaw and Allen, *Preaching in the Context of Worship*. See in particular the essay by Wilson in this volume, entitled "Preaching and the Sacrament of Holy Communion."

to homiletical theology because both are reflections on a practice. Liturgical theologians describe this method of theological reflection by making a distinction between "primary" and "secondary" liturgical theology. Primary liturgical theology, as Gordon Lathrop defines it, is "the communal meaning of the liturgy exercised by the gathering itself."[4] The assembly uses words and signs to speak of God, and thus engages in theology. Secondary liturgical theology is reflection on these words and signs; it is "discourse that attempts to find words for the experience of the liturgy and to illuminate its structures."[5] Alexander Schmemann outlines the tasks of secondary liturgical theology as finding the theological concepts that will express the fundamental nature of the liturgical experience, and then connecting those concepts with systematic theology, those ideas by which the Church expresses its doctrine and faith.[6] Thus liturgical theology stands between worship and dogmatics, and aims to explain the ancient rule of the Church: *lex orandi, lex credendi*. Liturgical theology emphasizes the *causal* nature of this relationship, that it is not just that the law of praying and the law of believing are related, but that the law of praying *dictates* the law of believing. Thus, Schmemann, Lathrop and others insist that "the ongoing tradition and actual performance of the liturgy [is] the primary source for the Church's theology," and see their task as liturgical theologians "to make the liturgical experience of the Church again one of the life-giving sources of the knowledge of God."[7]

Homiletical theology is a natural conversation partner to liturgical theology because it rests on a similar practical-theological method. Homiletical theology takes as its starting point the "primary theology" that emerges from sermon preparation and delivery, from which "secondary theology" is derived. From the primary theology expressed in the practice of preaching itself, homiletical theology develops secondary theology that reflects upon the practice in relationship to the doctrines of the Christian faith.

In addition to this similarity of method, sacramental theology as a subset of liturgical theology engages similar theological questions and *loci* to those raised about preaching as an event of divine self-revelation. Sacramental theology wrestles with the question of how God can be made known to us through material means. Even though the material means are not the same (bread and wine versus the human person and words of the preacher), the

---

4. Lathrop, *Holy Things*, 5.
5. Ibid., 6.
6. Schmemann, *Introduction to Liturgical Theology*, 17.
7. Morrill, *Bodies of Worship*, 5. Schmemann, *Introduction to Liturgical Theology*, 23. Aidan Kavanagh also argues for the liturgical event as primary theology. See his *On Liturgical Theology* (New York: Pueblo Publishing, 1984), 73–95.

theological claims made and issues raised are similar, and engage the same doctrinal *loci* as homiletical theology engages. Theologies of the sacraments wrestle with questions at the intersection of doctrines of revelation and theological anthropology, since they consider how it is that God is made known to humankind through material means. These questions open onto christology and ecclesiology, since what makes the sacraments a privileged place of divine self-revelation has to do with their grounding in God's primordial self-revelation in Christ, and in the commissioning of the church to be Christ's body in the world, and hence the primary sacrament of God's presence.[8] Homiletical theology can be in fruitful dialogue with sacramental theology in part because much of the work of wrestling with these questions and synthesizing these doctrines is already being done there, and the conversation in homiletics can build on such a synthesis.

Recent developments in sacramental theology make this conversation yet more fruitful, since there has recently been a shift toward thinking about the sacraments not primarily as objects that dispense grace, but as personal encounters between God and people. Relatedly, there has been a shift toward considering the entire liturgy as sacramental. Russian Orthodox liturgical theologian Alexander Schmemann maintains that the whole liturgy is a sacrament in that it reveals the essential sacredness of all creation and of human life; it is the fulfillment and manifestation of this world as God's world, of our life as participating in God's life. In this understanding, "a sacrament is primarily a revelation of the *sacramentality* of creation itself, for the world was created and given to man [sic] for the conversion of creaturely life into divine life."[9] A sacrament is both cosmic, referring to the world as God created it, and eschatological, looking forward to the fulfillment of this world in the kingdom of God.

The upshot of this argument is, first, to move away from ontological or metaphysical arguments about how material objects in the liturgy can become sacred. For Schmemann, the whole of the liturgy is sacramental not because some change or transubstantiation occurs in the physical elements of the service, but because in the liturgy the Church willingly participates in something that has already been given—namely, God's new life. This argument also emphasizes that the whole of the liturgy is sacramental, and that its sacramentality cannot be reduced to one moment when a material object transforms from being profane to being sacred. Rather, since all of the liturgy participates in the reality of God's kingdom, all of the liturgy is sacramental.

---

8. See Rahner's description of Jesus Christ as God's primordial sacrament, and the Church as God's basic sacrament, in *Foundations of the Christian Faith*, 412.

9. Schmemann, *The Eucharist*, 33.

All the rites of the liturgy are a progressive manifestation of the realities of Christ's saving work—not an accomplishment of these realities, since that has already been done. Thus Schmemann, in his volume dedicated to exploring the Eucharist, explicitly labels each section of the liturgy as a sacrament: the first chapter is the "sacrament of the assembly," followed by the "sacrament of entrance," and so on through all the sections of the service, including preaching, which he labels "the sacrament of the Word."[10] He entitles his chapters in this way so that throughout the book he can demonstrate how all parts of the liturgy function sacramentally, in that all parts of the liturgy reveal God's new life which has been given to us.

These shifts in understanding of the sacraments have the effect of including preaching as a sacramental event, inasmuch as it is part of the liturgy as a whole. Furthermore, this redefinition of what sacraments are holds promise for thinking about preaching as an event of divine-self-revelation, since one can theorize this event not according to metaphysical principles for how profane objects are transformed into sacred ones (the old way that sacramental theology operated), but rather in terms of how God enters into personal relationship with us (the new approach of sacramental theology). Since preaching is invariably personal, as God reveals Godself in relationship to the person of the preacher, this new emphasis on sacraments as events of personal encounter provides a helpful framework for analyzing preaching as sacramental.

One aspect of this shifting understanding of sacraments that is particularly helpful for theorizing preaching is the increased emphasis on the human bodies who participate in worship. Considering the liturgy as a whole to be sacramental means that the focus shifts from the mechanics of what is happening to the bread and wine at the altar to what is happening in the bodies of worshippers throughout the liturgy. How are the embodied selves of the gathered community being transformed, made holy, brought into relationship with God? Contemporary liturgical theologians emphasize that sacramental grace always comes to us through our bodies, and that liturgy emphasizes and enacts this truth. The recent volume, *Bodies of Worship*, for instance, focuses explicitly on the body's experience in worship, based on the premise that the body's experience in worship helps us to understand what worship really is and what is happening in it—how it is that worship connects us to God and to each other.[11] As Bruce Morrill, the volume's editor, notes, this focus on the bodiliness of liturgy brings liturgical theology into alignment with a growing interest in the body in post-modern scholarship, an interest generated in part because the body's "resistance to abstraction" serves the philosophical

---

10. Schemann, *The Eucharist*, 65–80.
11. Morrill, *Bodies of Worship*, 1, 3.

and political interests of this scholarship. Part of this scholarship has involved a critique or even rejection of the ways in which the Christian theological tradition has denigrated or discounted the body. However, liturgical theologians insist that the body is central to the Christian faith, because God in Jesus Christ became flesh and dwelt among us, accomplishing our salvation through the life, death, and resurrection of the very human body of Jesus of Nazareth, and thus that "God saves humanity right in our very material actions and circumstances," that is, in our very bodies.[12] As Louis-Marie Chauvet expresses it, "Faithful to its biblical roots, ecclesial tradition has attempted to discern what is most 'spiritual' in God on the basis of what is most 'corporeal' in us. This is especially the case in the liturgy. But it is more widely the case in the whole of *Church life*."[13]

As Morrill notes, the insistence that liturgy constitutes the Church's primary theology is consistent with a greater focus on embodiment—i.e., it is precisely because liturgy is a set of embodied practices that it is the basis for our theology, because it is above all in our embodied experience that we are brought into relationship to God: "there is no disembodied realm where we are being saved."[14] Thus, while contemporary liturgical theologies focus less on the mechanics of how material things are transformed to be bearers of grace, these theologies put great emphasis on the material and embodied nature of liturgy, operating from the principle that, "for Christians, the most spiritual of realities can only be experienced or known in and through the materiality of our bodies," and that this principle is powerfully encountered in sacramental worship.[15] The mystery of the sacraments is that material things, bread and wine, oil, water, can become bearers of God's grace. Sacramental grace always comes to us through our bodies, through eating and drinking, being washed, being anointed. Morrill also makes the crucial point that to focus on the body is inevitably to recognize that the body is never merely a physical body, for that body is embedded in and shaped by the various bodies of which it is a part, such as the Church as the body of Christ; the liturgical body, the community which participates in the worship together; and the cultural body, which is made up of various social relationships that influence the body's experience of itself.

Liturgical theology's methodological commitment to treat embodied practices as a primary wellspring of theological knowledge finds a parallel in much other recent theological scholarship, in which there is evidence of a

12. Ibid., 3.
13. Chauvet, *Symbol and Sacrament*, 111. Emphasis Chauvet's.
14. Morrill, *Bodies of Worship*, 4.
15. Ibid., 3.

"material turn." Formulations of doctrine, or theories of religion, increasingly take as their starting point not texts, but embodied and material existence.[16] This turn to embodied experience forms the basic methodological premise underlying the recent dogmatic scholarship of Sarah Coakley, for example. In her recent work on the doctrine of the Trinity, she argues that prayer, and especially contemplation, is the indispensable "matrix for trinitarian reflection," that "a particular set of bodily and spiritual practices (both individual and liturgical) are the *precondition* for trinitarian thinking of a deep sort." Putting the point negatively, Coakley insists that "if one is resolutely *not* engaged in the practices of prayer, contemplation, and worship, then there are certain sorts of philosophical insight that are unlikely, if not impossible, to become available to one."[17] Coakley points out that this is an "anti-foundationalist" position, in that her claim is that a secular, universalist rationality is not the uncontended basis for making theological claims, but rather theological claims rest on the knowledge gained through embodied spiritual practices. As Coakley puts it, "What distinguishes this position, then, from an array of other 'post-foundationalist' options that currently present themselves in theology, is the commitment to the discipline of *particular* graced bodily practices which, over the long haul, afford certain distinctive ways of knowing."[18] Coakley's methodology is similar to that of Morrill and other liturgical theologians in that she insists that theological knowledge arises from embodied spiritual and liturgical practices, that there are aspects of God's relationship to us, and of God in Godself, that we simply cannot know except through the body's experience.

Adopting this methodological priority given to embodied experience, I argue that the "primary homiletical theology" that takes place in the event of preaching is embodied theology, and that preaching experienced as a bodily action involving voice, breath, self, community, liturgical rite and liturgical space is a fruitful starting point for secondary homiletical-theological reflection on the meaning of preaching. Moreover, it is not only that the body's experience of preaching reveals what preaching is, but also that preaching, as a liturgical and therefore embodied act, is an event of primary theology that can become the basis for secondary theology in which we arrive at doctrinal truth about God, ourselves, and the two of us in relationship to each other. Just as Coakley argues that there are core Christian doctrines such as the doctrine of the Trinity that we only fully grasp through embodied practices and

---

16. Note, for instance, the "material turn" in studies of theology and religion, as noted in the 2015 AAR Call for Papers.

17. Coakley, *God, Sexuality, and the Self,* 16. Emphasis Coakley's.

18. Coakley, *God, Sexuality, and the Self,* 19. Emphasis Coakley's.

embodied knowledge, there are essential dimensions of Christian doctrine that we understand most fully when we experience them in the embodied event of preaching. In terms of a theology of promise, we come to understand and believe in God's promise to be present with us through the embodied experience of that fulfilled promise in preaching. This primary theological experience then becomes the basis for a secondary homiletical theology of promise.

Despite the fact that preaching is clearly an embodied activity, in which the preacher communicates her message through the engagement of her body in voice, movement, gesture, and by the body's presence on display before others, it is striking how infrequently the body is included in theorizing about preaching, or even in training for the practice of preaching. If the body is considered at all in most textbooks on preaching, it is in a late chapter of the book on techniques for "delivery" of the sermon. The starting point for theorizing about preaching is never the body; it is usually the biblical text, the tradition of the Church, or the incarnation of Jesus Christ. However, following liturgical theology's method, I argue that it is preaching experienced as a whole, as a bodily action involving voice, breath, self, community, liturgical rite and liturgical space, that ought to be the starting point for secondary theological reflection on the meaning of preaching. Preaching needs to be theorized as embodied and performative knowing of God. Out of that experience of God arises secondary reflection that seeks theological concepts to describe God accurately. Theologies of promise would thus take their starting point from the body's experience of God's fulfilled promise in the preaching event itself.

THE SACRAMENTAL STRUCTURE OF PREACHING

What, then, is the body's experience of God's fulfilled promise of presence in preaching? One way to answer this question is to look at the physical processes of speaking—that is, to explore what is happening in our bodies when we speak, and how in this speaking we may experience God's promised presence. For the outline of the physical steps involved in speaking, I am drawing on a method for training the speaking voice developed by voice teacher Kristin Linklater, which is widely used in the dramatic arts.[19] This method of vocal training takes students through a progression of physical and vocal exercises that are designed to free and strengthen the speaking voice. The fundamental premise of this method is that each person is born with a voice capable of ex-

---

19. Linklater's approach to voice training is outlined in: Linklater, *Freeing the Natural Voice*, and *Freeing Shakespeare's Voice*.

pressing, through a two-to-four-octave pitch range, the fullness of her thought and feeling. The way the voice works is that the speaker feels a need to communicate, the brain signals to the body, the need to communicate stimulates breathing muscles—abdominal muscles, diaphragm, rib muscles—and they expand to let breath in to communicate her thought and feeling; breath comes in, goes out, makes contact with vocal chords, vocal chords vibrate and sound results, amplified by resonators, articulated by lips and tongue. That is how the voice works when the speaker is a baby, where the voice expresses life-and-death need, and where the voice is intrinsically connected to the body. However, as the speaker grows up she learns that it is not always socially acceptable to express herself from the place of life-and-death need, so she learns that when she feels the desire to communicate, instead of letting that impulse travel down into the body, where deep need is felt, to reroute the impulse to a more socially acceptable place, the upper chest and throat. Through social conditioning, trauma, and the tensions of daily life she learns to detach her impulse to communicate from the diaphragm and abdominal muscles, and to express that impulse through the throat and face. The voice becomes disconnected from the body, unsupported by the breath, and is squeezed out by overworking the throat, jaw, and tongue muscles. Such speaking leads to the divorce of words from meaning and emotion, such that words describe rather than reveal their content. The speaker whose voice is thus distorted is no longer fully present in her communication. The range of the voice shrinks from 2–4 octaves to 3–4 notes of speaking range.

The purpose of the Linklater method is to rectify this situation by reconnecting speakers' voices to their bodies and emotions. Linklater's method of voice training takes students through a series of exercises which teach physical alignment, diaphragmatic breathing, relaxation of throat muscles, connecting voice with breath, and the use of the body's natural resonators to amplify the voice. The goal of the method is fully embodied communication, in which the voice and body are free, in which the words spoken exist not only in the head but are connected to and expressed through the whole body. When we speak with this freedom and connection, we are not just speaking words, but the words are living in our bodies; the meaning of the words is communicated in the words we speak. Our whole selves are communicating the words, and we are fully present in this act of communication.

This physical process of speaking, as it takes place in preaching, is not merely physical and technical, but is itself an event of primary theology, which can give rise to secondary theological reflection. One way to enter into secondary theological reflection on this physical process of speaking is to flesh out the implications of the claim that preaching is sacramental by comparing the liturgical action that takes place in preaching with the liturgical action that takes place in the Eucharist. Gregory Dix famously proposed that the action of the Eucharist was fourfold, corresponding to Jesus Christ's four actions at the institution of the Eucharist. The four actions were: to take the elements, to bless or give thanks to God for them, to break them (or pour them out), and to share them.[20] These four actions are embedded in the words of institution in contemporary Eucharistic prayers: "On the night before he died for us, our Lord Jesus Christ took bread; and when he had given thanks to you, he broke it, and gave it to his disciples and said, '"Take, eat."' Although the specifics of Dix's construal of the four-action shape of the Eucharist have been critiqued and revised, the essential fourfold shape of the Eucharistic action remains influential in liturgical thinking and practice.[21] I argue that each of these four Eucharistic actions in turn can be compared to a particular aspect of the physical process of speaking as outlined by Linklater, and that exploring this correlation illuminates how God fulfills God's promise to be present with us in preaching. The fourfold action of the Eucharist is the outline of the steps by which God is present to us in the Eucharistic meal; likewise, four aspects or steps in the process of speaking suggest the steps by which our voices and bodies become vessels of God's presence.

Of these four moments, the second moment is a focal point in the fulfillment of God's promise of presence. This moment, the *epiclesis* or blessing, is the moment when the Holy Spirit comes upon the elements, sanctifying them to be Christ's body and blood. Although, as liturgical theologians argue, the entire liturgy is sacramental, this moment crystallizes or brings into focus something that is happening throughout the liturgy, which is the meeting of the divine with the material, the heavenly and the earthly. It is significant that this meeting is accomplished through the coming of the Holy Spirit in particular. The Holy Spirit, in the Eucharist as elsewhere, is the person of the Trinity that draws us into relationship with God. Sarah Coakley describes the Spirit as breaking down the ontological gap between God and humankind, not by abolishing difference, but by investing it with participative mystery.[22] The *epiclesis*, the coming of the Holy Spirit upon the elements of bread and wine, is the paradigmatic liturgical event of the bridging of this ontological gap.

If preaching is sacramental, is it possible to locate an *epiclesis* in the preaching event? I suggest that the *epiclesis* in the Eucharist is analogous to

20. Dix, *The Shape of the Liturgy*, 78.

21. For a critique of Dix's four-action shape of the Eucharistic meal, see Wainwright, "Recent Eucharistic Revision," 332–33.

22. Coakley, *God, Sexuality, and the Self,* 330.

the preacher's moment-by-moment experience of the breath in the body, the breath that supports the voice. According to the Linklater method, the breath is the crucial element that forges the connection between the thoughts, feelings, and impulses we seek to communicate, and the authentic communication of these thoughts and feelings in the voice. It is the breath fueling the voice that brings this communication about, giving our words the ring of truth, making our words flesh.

This experience of breath in connection with the voice is a profound, often unconscious experience of primary theology; it is the lived experience of our relationship with God, of God's fulfillment of God's promise to be present with us, out of which we craft our secondary theologies of promise. It is not a coincidence that the Spirit is consistently described and imagined as the *ruach*, the *pneuma*, the very breath of God that moved over the face of the deep at creation and breathed the breath of life into the first human, the same breath that the risen Christ breathed on his disciples when he said, "Receive the Holy Spirit" (John 20:22). Generally speaking, we tend to think of the connection of Spirit with breath as a metaphor, but if we consider the experience of breathing, especially in connection with speaking, as an actual experience of our relationship with God, this becomes a moment of primary theology, giving rise to secondary theological reflection on the nature of our relationship with God and God's promise that is revealed in this embodied experience.

THE EPICLESIS IN PREACHING: THE FULFILLMENT OF GOD'S DIALECTICAL PRESENCE

Three aspects of the experience of breathing in particular provide grist for secondary theological reflection on the nature of God's promise. First, to breathe is actually a *passive* experience; rather than making ourselves breathe, it is more accurate to say that we *are breathed*. Most of the time, of course, we breathe without consciously focusing on the breath; and even when we bring awareness to the breath, if we simply relax the breathing muscles, the breath comes and goes of itself, in its own natural rhythm. We do not make it happen, but more accurately allow it to happen. Theologically, the passive nature of the human breath reminds us that the fulfillment of God's promise to be with us, to animate us moment by moment, is something we allow more than something we create or make happen. Relationship with God is a gift of grace, God's making good on God's promise to be with us, rather than a human creation.

In addition to being an experience of God's fulfilled promise, the breath in the body is also a primary theological event of connection and communion.

Experientially, the breath connects us to each other; the word "con-spiracy" literally means "breathing-together." Emmanuel Levinas develops the idea that speaking is a signaling of one's ethical responsibility to the other, and argues that in the signaling of this responsibility, God, the transcendent, "passes by." Levinas describes breathing as a crucial moment in the opening of the self to the other: one "frees oneself by breathing from closure in oneself," and "breathing is transcendence in the form of opening up."[23] For Levinas, any attempts to enclose ourselves in our inwardness, separating ourselves from the call of the other, are disrupted by the breath itself, which intrinsically opens us to the hearer, and to the transcendence that is inherently signaled in this relationship. In terms of a theology of promise, the primary theological event of breath-empowered speech leads to secondary theological reflection on the communal nature of God's promise. The eschatological fulfillment of God's promised reign of justice is not a fulfillment promised to individuals, but rather to a whole community, the whole commonwealth of God.

The inherently communal quality of the breath helps to alleviate the risk that sacramental presence in preaching is limited to simply the body of the preacher. If God's presence were realized only in the preacher, the charge of Donatism could readily be made against this argument, for the argument would seem to imply that the preacher, through the indwelling of the Spirit, becomes nothing less than Christ. To claim this would be to posit an idolatrous elision of divine-human difference. One way to counter this risk is to point to the graced nature of the encounter with God that is inherent in the passive nature of the breath. In addition, to claim that preaching is sacramental, without collapsing the person of the preacher into the person of Christ, it is crucial to grasp the radically relational subjectivity that the breath instantiates and even creates. It is this relational subjectivity that Levinas develops, in which the subject is never enclosed in a separate subjectivity, but is radically open to the other; moreover, as Levinas notes, it is the breath itself that signals this openness to the other. When this understanding of the Spirit-breath is applied to preaching, it becomes apparent that the body of the preacher serves as an icon, by means of which God's sacramental presence is realized in the entire assembly, which is the body of Christ in its totality. Indeed, the Spirit-breath, breathing in the preacher and in the listeners, is the agent that unites the assembly into the one body of Christ. It is not the preacher in herself that is the sacrament of God's presence, but rather the preacher in her intrinsic connection to the listeners who witnesses to the sacramentality of the whole congregation.

---

23. Levinas, *Otherwise Than Being, or Beyond Essence*, 180, 181.

In addition to being a lived experience of God's gracious presence, which is inherently communal, the breath can provide an embodied experience of the dialectical nature of God's promised presence. When we allow the breath to drop deep into our bodies, and to connect with our words, this experience can lead to a sense of calm, but can also connect us to thoughts and feelings that we tend to leave unexpressed. To breathe is to connect to a fuller sense of self than we might often be aware of; as the Linklater voice method demonstrates, to connect breath deep in the body is to connect to what we need to say from a primal place of life-and-death need. Again, from a theological point of view, this is not surprising. The Holy Spirit has brought disruption, challenge, and a goad toward prophetic utterance as often as She has brought calm and serenity. The disruptive effects of the Holy Spirit in the body of the preacher are analogous to the disruptions the Holy Spirit brings to worship in general, and to the Eucharistic celebration in particular. As Matthew Myer Boulton argues, the work of the Holy Spirit in worship is to intervene into the destitution of human worship, which is of itself unable to fitly glorify God. The Holy Spirit breaks into this human incapacity, functioning as a divine adversary that opposes and transforms the poverty of our worship.[24]

The disruptive effects of the coming of the Spirit-breath into the body of the preacher highlight the dialectical nature of God's presence in preaching, and point to the dialectic in theologies of promise generally—the ways in which God's promise both has and has not been realized. In one sense the experience of the Spirit-breath in the body is the experience of God's promised presence fulfilled. Yet this same Spirit-breath points us toward an eschatological future that has not yet been fully realized, just as God's presence in the Eucharist is a fulfilled promise that at the same time points us forward toward a fuller eschatological realization of that promise. Bruce Morrill makes this point in maintaining that Schmemann's strong emphasis on liturgy as sacrament leads to a too "realized" eschatology, in that Schmemann understands liturgy as the place of pure *parousia*, pure revelation of God.[25] Conversely, Schmemann views the rest of the world as the place where there are no signs of the Kingdom of God, a place seemingly devoid of the sacred. Morrill argues that this position does not adequately take into account that God's presence in liturgy too is dialectical, that God can be hidden in liturgy (or *by* liturgy) as well as in the rest of the world.[26] Conversely, there are signs of the Kingdom of God in history and in human culture outside of the liturgy, signs that might be lacking in the liturgy itself. Chief among these signs are the cries of

24. Boulton, "The Adversary," 76.
25. Morrill, *Anamnesis as Dangerous Memory*, 192.
26. Ibid., 135.

the suffering and the oppressed, summoning the Church to do the work of God in the world by acting for justice. Liturgy can hide this aspect of God's reign precisely when it is posited as the place of full revelation, of the fulfilled promise of God's presence. This conviction turns the Church inward in satiation, not outward toward the world in longing for the complete fulfillment of the Kingdom of God in history as well as in liturgy. The collapse of the future into the present in Schmemann's doctrine of the Eucharist, his too-realized eschatology there, is apolitical in that it fails to take account of the suffering of the oppressed and the need to act for justice in history. It emphasizes God's presence as a promise fulfilled, rather than as pointing us forward to a fuller realization of that promise.

As a corrective to the over-realized eschatology he finds in Schmemann's theology of liturgy, Morrill connects Johannes Metz's concept of "dangerous memory" to the *anamnesis* that takes place in the Eucharist, arguing that to conceive of liturgy as *anamnesis*, a dangerous memory of Christ, is to maintain liturgy's eschatological thrust more fully than Schmemann does. *Anamnesis* is eschatological because it looks forward to the fullness of what God will do, based on the memory of what God has already done in Christ. Such memory interrupts the flow of evolutionary time and the hegemony of modernity, bringing to light the suffering of the oppressed through the memory of Christ's passion. In this sense liturgy interrupts the rest of life; but by the same token liturgy itself is interrupted by the memory of Christ, which is God's call to remember those who suffer today. Morrill, himself a Roman Catholic, notes that "the discussion of the Eucharistic celebration in terms of an intervening moment, an interruption in time, might come as a challenge to Roman Catholics, for whom theological and pious reflection on the sacrament has long been dominated by a narrowly focused notion of real presence." Sounding like Barth and the Reformers, Morrill maintains that real presence is not a static thing; rather, "the eucharistic celebration is an *encounter* with the saving presence of God."[27] *Anamnesis* is not mere memory of a past event, but the basis of a genuine encounter with God in the present, since "Jesus' words over the bread and cup, along with his command for his followers to perform this ritual, constitute a promise of presence to them, in the mutual act of divine and human remembrance."[28]

Morrill insists, moreover, that "Christians' genuine perception (and thus, appropriation) of the reality of Christ's presence in the Eucharist depends upon their (practical) awareness of the reality of the suffering in their

---

27. Ibid., 175.
28. Ibid., 178.

historical midst."²⁹ In order for the sacrament to be fully realized, in other words, it needs to be interrupted by the memory of something outside of it, so that, here again, real presence is not something statically given in certain physical elements, but depends on relationship—between God and the worshipper, and between the liturgy and the rest of existence. The presence of Christ in the sacraments is a proleptic presence, which points forward toward a reign of justice that has not yet been fully realized. The dialectic of God's promise, its status as both "already" and "not yet" realized, is instantiated in the Eucharist itself.

Analogously, the coming of the Spirit-breath into the body of the preacher is potentially also a moment of *anamnesis*, a dangerous memory of Christ's passion that also brings to light the suffering of the oppressed today. It is an encounter with God's saving presence, the fulfillment of God's promise of presence; this is never a static presence, but is always pointing us forward to God's promised reign of justice which has not yet been fully realized. In a sense, the sermon is interrupted by the Spirit's coming and by the dangerous memory She provokes of suffering and of redemption. This is one way to describe the disruptive effect of the Spirit breathing in the preacher, summoning her to speak dangerous words that stir up the calm waters of liturgy, preventing the experience of God's presence there from turning to satiety or complacency. In this way, preaching itself is interrupted by the Holy Spirit, and becomes in turn an interruption into liturgy.

The reality and memory of suffering interrupt liturgy, such that liturgy cannot be seen as pure *parousia*. Preaching is a primary place where this interruption takes place; it is a moment when *anamnesis*, dangerous memory can arise. Preaching can be an event in liturgy that breaks liturgy open, raising the cries of the suffering and giving voice to eschatological longing. Morrill argues that preaching is one crucial place in the liturgy where participants come to know and appropriate "the Christian faith in an 'anticipatory memory' of both crisis and consolation."³⁰ Preaching has an "anamnetic character," as it presents the congregation with scriptural "narratives which at times gently invite and at other times strongly demand a decision to enter into God's life, to take up the way of imitation."³¹ The preacher's task is to "throw together the worlds of Scripture and the contemporary community in the unique moment of a particular liturgical celebration." This "throwing together," which is the root meaning of the term "symbol," constitutes the sermon as a liturgical act, symbolic in that it unites two apparently dissimilar realities (Scripture and

---

29. Ibid., 185.
30. Ibid., 201.
31. Ibid., 211.

contemporary life) to show their essential relatedness.[32] As Morrill's argument suggests, liturgy is not always self-interpreting; it needs preaching in order to jolt it out of a too-realized eschatology, a sense that the Kingdom of God has already come in its fullness. In this sense preaching is not only *part* of liturgy but an *interruption* into liturgy, or a *corrective* to liturgy.[33] Preaching thus becomes a signal of the dialectical quality of God's promise in general, how that promise is given and yet hidden, inaugurated and yet not fully realized, in liturgy as in life.

Preachers experience this interruption that preaching is in the interruption that the Spirit-breath makes into preaching itself. Thus, in the very act of speaking we are drawn into an experience of God's promise, experiencing the dialectical nature of this promise. On the one hand, the Spirit-breath breathing within us is the fulfillment of God's promise to be with us, just as the *epiclesis* of the bread and wine is the fulfillment of God's promised presence. At the same time, this same Spirit's coming, both in the body of the preacher and upon the material elements at the table, disrupts any notions of static divine presence, connecting us back to the radical challenge of Jesus' person and work, and also driving us forward toward God's eschatological reign of justice. The presence of God in the preached word is always a proleptic presence that directs us toward a future fulfillment of God's promise. As preachers, we can sense this in the breath itself, perhaps especially in moments of the greatest destitution in our preaching, when the "sufferings of this present time" (Rom 8:18) seem like they occlude God's promise entirely. In those moments, Paul reminds us that in our weakness "the Spirit intercedes with sighs too deep for words." (Rom 8:26). These very sighs, even if they be sighs of weakness or despair, are the action of the Spirit in us, opening us to a future promise that we cannot perhaps sense, but toward which the Spirit is leading us. Thus, the Spirit-breath opens our words and our presence beyond our words to the sometimes wordless sighs of prophecy.

CONCLUSION

Homiletical theology begins from the premise that preaching is not merely the application of theological truths generated elsewhere, but rather that

---

32. Ibid., 211.

33. J. J. Von Allmen makes a similar argument to Morrill's that the importance of the sermon is that it turns the congregation outward, connecting the life of the Church to the life of the world. Thus, the balance of word and table prevents "liturgical escapism and anchorless prophetic activity." Allmen, *Preaching and Congregation*, 32. Quoted in Noren, "The Word of God in Worship," 42.

preaching is itself an exercise in theological method, and is generative of theological reflection. This paper seeks to apply this theological method to the embodied experience of preaching, and to tease out the theological claims related to God's promise that can be derived from this experience. Placing these reflections in dialogue with liturgical theology, I compare the event of preaching with the four-fold action of the Eucharist, and specifically focus on the experience of the breath as analogous to the *epiclesis*. The coming of the Holy Spirit as breath in the body of the preacher is an event of primary theology that gives rise to secondary theological reflection on several aspects of God's promise. First, the Spirit-breath in the preacher's body signals the graced nature of God's promise—that it is something we receive rather than something we create of ourselves. Second, the Spirit-breath in the preacher's body points to the proleptic nature of God's promised presence—that this divine promise is yet to be fully realized, and will be realized only as the sufferings of this present time give way to future glory. Finally, the Spirit-breath in the body of the preacher instantiates the inherently communal nature of God's promise, both as it is realized in the moment of preaching, and as it is yet to be fulfilled in God's in-breaking reign.

What I hope to have suggested in these investigations is the promise of homiletical theology itself. Homiletical theology takes preaching seriously as generative of theological knowledge. To do this is to take seriously knowledge of God that is embodied and performative—to ask what speaking bodies know about God's promise, for instance, and to take this knowledge as foundational to further theological reflection, rather than as tangential to it. Such bodily knowledge has the potential not only to confirm, but also to amplify, challenge, and significantly augment the claims we make about God's promise, as well as numerous other aspects of our knowledge of God.

—4—

A Homiletical Theology of Promise
More Than One Genre?

—Paul Scott Wilson

Homiletical theology, of which this chapter is an example, has a form, content, style, and function—features that commonly mark a genre. The form is an academic essay, the content is theological matters relating to preaching and teaching preaching, the style is defined by *The Chicago Manual of Style*, and the function is to engage informed conversation. Homiletical theology is rooted in the Bible and European academic traditions and makes theological and ethical claims much like other theology and is written for preachers and academic peers. All of this is good and well, but from time to time most homileticians have also encountered another form (or forms) of what could also be called homiletical theology that has a different function/s. As a genre, it lies somewhere between the academic essay and the sermon, it borders the region of popular and devotional literature yet it is sophisticated, specialized, poetical, and theological, and for the most part lacks critical attention. It too relies on Bible and tradition and has some marks of academic writing. What makes it distinctive is that, unlike most of our formal writing, it follows the conversational style, language, and use of imagery and plot that homiletics in recent decades has advocated for the pulpit. Both types exist to serve and strengthen the pulpit, but this second genre pays special attention to clarity and simplicity, creativity and experience, and offers what is arguably a more integrated or holistic approach to the topics it addresses.

For convenience, we will call the first form academic and the second form poetic (even though this second form has flexible boundaries and may include hybrid forms). Here we will consider these two forms of homiletical theology by focusing on a common topic, a theology of promise. We will explore what the two forms have in common, mainly in terms of Bible and theology, and then turn to poetics and rhetoric, two areas in which they seem distinct.

COMMON FEATURES OF BOTH KINDS OF HOMILETICAL THEOLOGY ON THE SUBJECT OF PROMISE

Bible

The Bible is an appropriate foundation for both preaching and homiletical theology. One could argue that the purpose of the sermon is to render God's past promises in the present day. Preaching is rooted in God's faithfulness to those promises throughout history, in the ongoing fulfillment of those promises in the present and future, and in their ultimate fulfillment at the end of time, which the resurrection of Jesus Christ anticipates. The sermon need not just report about God's promises in the past, nor simply recite the content of those promises, the sermon ideally can be the embodied event of those promises in the present. When the sermon functions as the Word of God, people may listen with the expectation of hearing God speak. Several of us in homiletics argue that ideally the sermon moves beyond teaching to proclamation, to loving, saving, liberating words of good news now for the current listeners in the particularity of their various social and cultural contexts.[1] In this view, the sermon is in large part an act of God, and it is by this act that the congregation finds its relationship with the living God renewed. In the experience of God in the now, promises of the past are reiterated, Christ is perceived as the present and ultimate fulfillment of those promises, and they are held out as true for this time and place. While the sermon may be based in all manner of biblical texts with various messages, the sermon is fundamentally promissory by its nature as a saving vehicle of God. It is promissory not least because Christ commissioned preaching, because he promised to be present "wherever two of three are gathered in my name," and because of the presence of the Spirit

---

1. Wilson, *Setting Words on Fire*.

in gathering the church and sending it forth to help fulfill the promises God has made.

Homiletical theology grows in the same rich soil as the sermon. There is no fence between the two. Like the sermon itself and rooted in the Bible, it is likewise promissory communicating the nature of God and the content of God's past promises.[2] A promise is an agreement, assurance, pledge, or commitment on the part of someone or some organization to do something. The most obvious forms of promise in the Bible are God's covenants with humanity. These can be conditional as in the covenants with Moses (esp., Deut 11:26–28) and Israel in relation to the land (Deut 30:1–9), involving an "if/then" formula and a blessing or curse, each party holding responsibilities and duties. Israel, for its part, promises to live by the commandments and laws God has given. On the other hand, unconditional covenants are simple promises of undeserved favor and grace, as in Noah (esp., Gen 8:20–9:17), Abraham (Gen 12:1–3), David (2 Sam 7:8–16), and the new covenant prophesied by Jeremiah 31:31, claimed to be fulfilled in Jesus Christ as the "new covenant in my blood" (Luke 22:20, Matt 26:28, Mark 14:24, Heb 8:7–13, 10:29). Both types of covenant are an expression of God's love, redemption, sustenance, and protection. They are expressions of who God is.

Homiletical theology to my mind is God-centered, rooted in creation, Easter, in the promise that believers are "a new creation" (2 Cor 5:17), and in Christ's return at the end of time. The faithful today look to Christ as the fulfillment of the law (Matt 5:17; Romans 3), and to the gift of the Spirit in forming the church at Pentecost. They live into the promise in the present, in the church as Christ's body, in the sacraments as present participation in Christ's death and resurrection, in the accompaniment and empowerment of the Spirit to do what is required by the law, namely acts of justice, mercy, and righteousness.

Preaching is promissory. Michael Knowles says that it involves dying and rising, as Jesus says in John 12:24, "Very truly, I tell you, unless a grain of wheat falls into the earth and dies, it remains just a single grain; but if it dies, it bears much fruit."[3] Through preaching, Christians live into specific promises that await their final fulfillment. These include: the wolf dwelling with the lamb and no one hurting or destroying (Isa 11:6–9); justice rolling down "like

---

2. Gordon Lathrop in liturgical studies speaks of liturgy as primary theology and reflection on it as secondary. See Lathrop, *Holy Things*, 5. Ruthanna B. Hooke in the current volume uses the same distinction. A key difference between our two approaches is that I would not preclude homiletical theology in its range of genres from proclamation or from being primary theology at times.

3. Knowles, *Of Seeds and the People of God*, 2015. See also Rom 6:4; Gal 2:20.

waters, and righteousness like an ever-flowing stream" (Amos 5:34); and every tear wiped away, all things made new, and death no more (Rev 21:4–5).

Both preaching and homiletical theology communicate the specificity of these promises as they arise out of particular biblical texts. In the history of preaching, the single-most common purpose of preaching, irrespective of denomination, is the promise of salvation for individual souls. Jesus promised, "For God so loved the world that he gave his only Son, that everyone who believed in him may not perish but may have eternal life." (John 3:16; 1 John 2:17.) In recent times, other purposes have come more to the fore, often in a broadened understanding that salvation is intimately related to corporate life and social justice. These purposes draw on positive promises of Jesus, for instance concerning the importance of loving one's neighbor as oneself (Matt 22:39; Mark 12:31; Luke 10:27); being merciful (Matt 5:7) and working for peace (Matt 5:9); welcoming the stranger, as in "I was a stranger . . . " (Matt 25:35) and the Good Samaritan (Luke 10:25–37); bringing good news to the poor and freeing the oppressed (Luke 4:18); and, whatsoever "you did to the least of these . . . you did to me" (Matt 25:40). All of the above are marks of God's actions in the present and the in-breaking of God's Realm. The purposes of preaching also draw on Jesus' threats or what some might call negative promises, like the "woe to you" passages (Luke 6:24–26) and the rich man and Lazarus (Luke 16:19–31); the weeds among the wheat (Matt 13:24–30, 36–43; Mark 4:1–20), the punishment of those who do not recognize Christ in their midst (Matt 25:41–46), the signs of the end of the age (Matt 24); and other eschatological texts like 1 Thes 5:1–11; 2 Thes 1:7–10, 2:1–12, and the Book of Revelation.

To what degree are biblical studies and homiletical theology aligned? Several decades ago scholars might have been surprised at the question even being asked, so obvious was the assumed answer. Today the answer must be more guarded. First, homiletics has taken a theological turn,[4] and to the degree that this is true, there is need in the pulpit for focus on God and the good news of God's saving actions, either "in or behind the biblical text," as I like to put it. This is not a focus of most biblical studies, which is to say that while many hermeneutical lenses are commonly employed in examining texts, one that focuses on the divine is not typically employed unless a specific text mentions God.

Second, the direction of biblical studies today is not consistently towards the pulpit. In 2004, one scholar assessing the future of biblical studies lamented "the growing compartmentalization and overspecialization of most graduate

---

4. Jacobsen, "Introduction," 4.

programs, and their over-emphasis on methods rather than text-skills"[5]. He added, "even when biblical scholars are talking about the same passage, their presuppositions are so different, they can hardly talk to each other."[6] Perhaps not much has changed. A 2012 study of biblical studies found that, "Instead of focusing on various slices of the Bible, (ancient) historical periods, or different methodologies, we have opted to differentiate in terms of geopolitics and culture . . . matters such as the global division of labor, patterns of exploitation, and issues related to gender and race."[7] Other scholars in 2015 speak of a "post-linguistic turn" in biblical studies, in which the focus has largely shifted from texts to methods: "the linguistic turn maintains that language does not merely reflect an a priori reality; rather, language creates and structures reality in concrete historical and social locations. For proponents of the linguistic turn, there is no 'reality' outside of expressions in language."[8] Critical questions of this sort can serve the study of the New Testament and related literature. Some of these questions may be of relevance to the pulpit, like the value of non-ecclesial interpretation of biblical texts or the significance of social and cultural location of readers in matters of exegesis. Others questions may be a distance from what can be commonly preached, including whether access to the ancient worlds or to the origin of Christianity is possible through such texts, and whether past and present can in fact relate. The pulpit and homiletical theology remain helpfully focused on textual analysis, hermeneutics, literary and theological content, and on matters of intertextuality or echoes that bring the gospel and the larger faith story to the fore.

Theology

Within homiletics, homiletical theology has emerged as a distinct area of interest mainly within the last two decades. Theologies of the Word had been a major focus of systematic theology into the 1960s, in the writings for instance of Reformed theologians like Karl Barth and Emil Brunner, and Lutherans like Gerhard Ebeling, Paul E. Scherer, and others. Perhaps they wrote too much—they may have seemed to have said everything that needed to be said—for whatever reasons, in more recent decades, academic study of the Word often became neglected. Douglas John Hall in his, *Professing the Faith*, mentioned

---

5. Brettler, "The Future of Biblical Studies."
6. Loc. cit.
7. Boer and Segovia, "Introduction: The Futures of Biblical Pasts," xvi.
8. Lopez and Penner, "Emerging Approaches in New Testament Studies," line 36–38.

preaching only in passing.[9] In general, theologies rooted in the experiences of the marginalized and oppressed became a new sun around which theological thoughts orbited, to considerable social benefit. By the 1990s there was a need to refocus on preaching as a theological task and that job often fell to homileticians.

A homiletical theology of promise necessarily draws on reflection from constructive and systematic theologians as well as homileticians. Several cautions are relevant. Theologians remind us, first, that Christian hope is not to be confused with having all our desires fulfilled. We are "resident aliens" and we live in a place that is not our true home.[10] Our hope is in the Triune God. The promise is that through Christ, all things will be reconciled to God (Col 1:20). Our ministry is a part of that reconciliation, a participation in the new creation that has both already begun and is in the future. John H. Leith warns that in terms of history, humans can hope for too much or too little[11]: "As long as human beings are creatures of instinct and impulse with the power and the freedom of self-transcendence, and as long as God continues to deal with human beings as . . . in the past, the possibilities of the future will include both good and evil. The possibilities for good are great and indeterminate, but there is no utopia."[12] Leith implies that the reign of God is only complete beyond history in the new heaven and new earth (Rev 21:1).[13]

Douglas John Hall expresses a second caution about hope and the end times: the promises of God are not about the immediate absence of struggle and pain, but are rather an invitation to deeper trust and faith:

> For, in contrast to either *optimistic* or *pessimistic* credos, Christian eschatology demands of us the kind of openness to the future that is able to hold together honest recognition of time's negating dimensions and an expectancy based on trust in the God who "gives life to the dead and calls into existence the things that do not exist" (Rom 4:17). It asks us to be realistic about the tragedy of existence while trusting that the end of the matter is "beyond tragedy" (Niebuhr).[14]

There is a dialectical tension between "time's negating dimensions" and the hope, and the latter is known in both the beginning and end of time in

---

9. Hall, *Professing the Faith*, 1993.
10. Hauerwas and Willimon, *Resident Aliens*, 2014.
11. Leith, *Basic Christian Doctrine*, 289.
12. Ibid., 292.
13. Ibid., 303.
14. Hall, *Professing the Faith*, 469.

the One who is the Alpha and Omega. This is true in each glimpse we have of God's in-breaking realm. Marianne Micks spoke of "the future present" in which we taste the end times already now in worship, centered around Word and table.[15] In worship, time and space are transcended. Chronological time (*chronos*) coincides with God's opportune time (*kairos*), that bears with it the saving nature of the eschaton. At the table, worshipers gather with Christ and with all the saints who have come before us and who will yet come after, and with all other Christians in the world.

A third caution concerns the negative or apocalyptic promises that have the capacity to strike terror even into faithful followers of Christ. Justice will come, and this is good and hopeful news. However, if we were all to receive our just deserts, few if any of us could stand. David Buttrick calls for preachers to use restraint with the kind of warnings issued in 1 Thessalonians. He points to 5:9–10, "For God has destined us not for wrath but for obtaining salvation through our Lord Jesus Christ, who died for us, so that whether we are awake or asleep, we may live with him." Buttrick notes, "The conventional language of apocalyptic rings out, and the Thessalonians have heard it before—all the talk of night and day, asleep and awake, thief in the night is nothing new. But then, in a single, sweet sweeping verse it's blown to bits by grace."[16] He adds, "In the passage the Bible is busy rewriting itself . . . Our task in the present time is to preach the awesome, incomprehensible love of God, declaring the boundaries of a kingdom wide as time and space and, yes, as wide as God's mercy."[17]

Of course, these days, threats or negative promises come not just from the Bible, they lurk behind nearly every major social and political issue and homiletical theology needs to be aware of them. Even as I write, an opinion column in *The New York Times* has the title, "A New Dark Age Looms," and warns how climate change may eventually render obsolete many of the understandings of our planet that humans now use to guide future planning.[18] Thus a fourth caution is this: any hope must take account of the tremendous suffering, sin, and brokenness in the world. The Christian message must take seriously the implications of inequality, racism, sexism, oppression, food and water shortages, non-renewable energy consumption, nuclear dangers, floods, rising seas, wars, and the like. So many things require urgent attention that James H. Cone once said, "The idea of heaven is irrelevant for Black Theology.

---

15. Micks, *The Future Present*, 1970.
16. Buttrick, *Preaching the New and the Now*, 62.
17. Ibid., 62–63.
18. Gail, "A New Dark Age Looms." *New York Times*, April 19, 2016.

The Christian cannot waste time contemplating the next world."[19] Hope can be constrained in other ways. Carol Christ says so many people suffer limited freedom that "it might seem meaningless to speak about creative freedom to them or, worse, insensitive to their real needs."[20]

Eschatology, as a theological subject, has itself come under suspicion in some quarters, not least because it can be used to put off social change. As Catherine Keller quipped, "Deferral, of course, is the stuff of eschatology . . ."[21] Other scholars note, "Many Christian feminists are highly suspicious of eschatology, arguing that in its most individualistic form it reflects a particularly male concern with the independent, isolated self and has contributed to towards the ecological crisis,"[22] concluding that, "personal salvation is not of the utmost importance in the world as we see it today, cosmic resurrection is, and it is a task that we all have to undertake as co-redeemers of creation."[23]

Christians must act to be good stewards of the earth and commit themselves to acting for the well-being of all people and creation as a whole. This responsibility is not lessened by the knowledge that the future is never entirely up to us. Our role is important, but grace is God's action, and while God enrolls, empowers, and delights in human actions that further God's purposes, our actions participate in saving initiatives begun by God. Emily Pennington urges, "We should not, however, overestimate the capabilities of human progression. I find it difficult to believe that the creation of freedom for all is within the realms of human possibility. Nor should we romanticize human progression."[24] We nonetheless assert an outcome that rests in the identity of God. The promises of God mean something precisely because they do take into account all the negative possibilities for the future and the depth of human sin and brokenness. As Pennington says, "God . . . desires, intends, and *will bring about* such a future [of liberation]. Such a perspective places hope in the very real presence of God enabling and empowering our struggles for freedom now, even as it looks toward a future where not one of these struggles will have been in vain."[25]

---

19. Cone, *Black Theology and Black Power*, 125. For a brief review of how Cone's thought has changed in appreciation of a role for eschatological vision in struggles for liberation see, Evans, *We Have Been Believers*, 172–75.

20. Carol Christ, *She Who Changes*, 179.

21. Keller, *Apocalypse Now and Then*, xiii.

22. Althaus-Reid and Isherwood, *Controversies in Feminist Theology*, 117.

23. Ibid., 124.

24. Pennington, "Does Feminism Need the Future?," 224.

25. Ibid., 226.

Such claims can be made not merely because we humans grieve the suffering we see around us, but because God does (Gen 6:6) and has promised to redeem creation. Throughout the Bible God makes liberating promises. God cannot be other than true to these promises ("if a house is divided against itself . . ." Mark 3:25), and Jesus Christ in his resurrected glory, together with the gift of the Spirit, is the promise of that. Henry H. Knight, III, recently reclaimed a phrase first used by Gordon Rupp in 1952. He described John Wesley's theology as an "optimism of grace." This is in contrast to both a "pessimism of nature" that affirms God will save only a small portion of humanity, and to "an optimism of nature"[26] that denies the fact of sin. An "optimism of grace" considers that, "given the limitations inherent in existence in a body in a fallen world, we dare set no limit to what the Grace of God can do . . . here and now."[27] These present saving acts are the work of the Spirit. Keller notes an irony, "the Spirit does the work of the Trinity without the prestige. It would not seem coincidental, then, that the Spirit carries all manner of feminine grammatical and metaphoric associations."[28]

A key question for homiletical theology and preachers is how the promises of God are to be delivered in sermons. James Kay speaks of preaching as "promissory narration"[29]:

> While the turn of the ages has occurred in the cross-resurrection of Jesus Christ, and the church has been established as its bridgehead, and the Holy Spirit has been given as the "guarantee" of God's final victory (2 Cor 1:22, 5:5) and the eschatological "goods" of God's rule (justification, sanctification, reconciliation, etc.) are now all on the scene, nevertheless, all has "not yet" happened.[30]

Promissory narration adds something to the narration advocated by postliberalism by accounting for "the self-involving agency of God as the ultimate Subject of sermonic discourse"[31] and by rendering the narrative identity of "Jesus Christ in his unsubstitutable particularity."[32]

---

26. Knight, *Anticipating Heaven Below*, 17. He cites Rupp, *Principalities and Powers*, 91–92.

27. Ibid., 18. Citing Rupp, 98.

28. Keller, *Apocalypse Now and Then*, 283.

29. Kay borrows this term from Morse, *The Logic of Promise in Moltmann's Theology*. See Kay, *Preaching and Theology*, 122, 125.

30. Ibid., 122.

31. Ibid., 125.

32. Ibid., 125. Kay notes that this goes on in the liturgical context of the church and need not be the weekly focus of the sermon, as long as the promises are preached.

The trouble/grace school of homiletics[33] is clear about preaching the promises. It stresses, among other things, that the purpose of preaching is not to preach a text, essential though that is, but to preach the gospel and the larger faith story from the perspective of a particular text. Gospel can be understood as the saving actions of God anywhere in the Bible and seen especially in Jesus Christ. The sermon mirrors the larger faith story in moving from trouble to grace, yet both are true, and they are reconciled only in faith. What Henry H. Mitchell and Frank A. Thomas speak about as celebration, often ending the sermon, becomes itself a form of interactive congregational participation in the proclaimed promises of God.[34]

DISTINGUISHING FEATURES OF POETIC HOMILETICAL THEOLOGY

Academic and poetic homiletical theologies share the above concern with biblical and theological promise. Poetic homiletical theology may be said to have an additional or more intentional concern with poetics and rhetoric.

A Concern for Poetics

Poetics is the study of matters related to aesthetics; form, function, and content; language and imagery; narrative, poetry, genre, plot, and the like. Ordinary speech has its own poetics, for instance in characteristic patterns of speech, vocabulary, imagery, and regional penchant for storytelling. Poetics as we use it here is intentional and artful departure from what is common. Academic homiletical theology has an art but it is largely unconcerned with aesthetics. Its interest in poetics is secondary, and might relate to the beauty, emotional appeal, and spirituality of biblical texts and how these matters affect and how texts communicate. Its purpose is communicating its subject matter according to established standards that give priority to information and specialized conversation. It is mainly concerned with teaching and demonstrating knowledge.

Might there be some advantage if homiletical literature were more concerned with the what and how of its own communication process? Might homiletics be more supportive of the pulpit if more often it shared and even modeled the kind of writing and speaking it hopes to foster?

---

33. Wilson, *Preaching and Homiletical Theory*, 87–115.
34. Mitchell, *Celebration and Experience in Preaching*, 2008 [1990]); Thomas, *They Like to Never Quit Praisin' God*, 1997.

Augustine, citing Cicero, said that preaching should "teach, delight and persuade." He added, "To teach is a necessity, to delight is a beauty, and to persuade is a triumph."[35] Of these three, delight connects most readily to poetics. The aim of delight is to affect the will of listeners and how they think and feel about a topic. Augustine identifies three styles, plain, moderate, and grand. He associates delight with a moderate style that is ornate and material that is carefully or artistically crafted. By contrast, teaching seeks clarity, thus it needs a plain or subdued style, using little flare and a minimum of metaphor and imagery. Persuasion in his view involves motivating listeners and requires proof together with the passion of the grand style.[36] These styles were more obvious in Latin than in English. Even at that, the styles overlap and one can imagine that some form of delight might be part of each style. George Campbell, in 1776, linked delight with "pleas[ing] the imagination."[37] Robert S. Reid thinks the recovery of narrative in the last half century is a recovery of the moderate style.[38] The grand style today might be seen in the impassioned speech of proclamation,[39] often connected with celebration in much African American preaching.

Historically the delight part of Augustine's teach, persuade, and delight trio has fit least comfortably with the church. Preaching in history was generally too serious a task for much encouragement of imagination, humor, or delight. Delight was dismissed as mere entertainment, pandering to the public tastes, and could be seen to conflict with the sober and urgent need for repentance and salvation.

A few notable styles in preaching history have been particularly open to delight. The plain style of the Puritans metaphysical preachers was plain in being stripped of images, yet was often filled with points and overly refined points and sub-points, obscure wordplays, and Latin puns that in their time delighted their listeners with their display of wit, though to our minds some of these sermons seem anything but delightful. To us they are likely to sound pretentious and artificial, playing to a wealthy educated elite of the era. Some Southern folk and African American preaching regularly made use of delight in bold imagery, fresh ideas, and musicality as in "The Sun Do Move" by John

---

35. Augustine, *On Christian Doctrine*, 136 (4.12.27). He cites Cicero's *Orator* 21:69.

36. On styles, see: Augustine, 137 (4.12.28); 143 (4.17.34).

37. Campbell cited by Loscalzo, "Rhetoric," in Willimon and Lischer, *Concise Encyplopedia of Preaching*, 411.

38. Robert S. Reid in an email conversation in 2007.

39. See Wilson, *Setting Words on Fire*, esp. 81–247. In addition to contrasting teaching and proclamation, this volume identifies three trouble genres of proclamation in the Bible and sermon history, and six grace genres, including celebration.

Jasper. More commonly, what C. F. W. Walther said in the nineteenth century still rings true: preachers are to preach condemnation and repentance to sinners. They are also to preach the sweet and comforting words of the gospel to those who are saved, but not in such a way that unrepentant sinners would in any way confuse such words as being directed at them.[40] There is no delight for the wicked.

In the history of preaching there have been various turns to poetics, whenever there has been a shift in style or approach, and some stand out: the metrical homily traditions of Romanos the Melodist, Ephrem and John of Damascus;[41] the metaphysical preaching of John Donne and others, and notably his *Devotions Upon Emergent Occasions* (1624); the emphasis in the mid 1800s on English Romantic ideas of imagination and organic form, function, and content in Horace Bushnell[42] and in character studies in several of the sermons of Frederick W. Robertson;[43] and celebration and other forms of proclamation in much African American and other preaching. The most recent recovery of poetics for the pulpit in the New Homiletic coincided with a new emphasis on art and story seen in the culture at large with the growth of mass media, movies, and advertising beginning in the 1950s.

What might poetic homiletical theology look like? One place we might look is H. Davis' 1958 poem, "Design for a Sermon."[44] It stands as a convenient marker of the (re-)turn to poetics and aesthetics in homiletics. His poem may have even more significance in retrospect than it had in its own time, because it effectively identified, anticipated, and modeled many Romantic understandings that became central for the New Homiletic. Davis began his poem with a notion of organic growth, "A sermon should be like a tree" in which form, content, and function all are connected, working toward a single unity. Thus, if we were to follow him, our topic of homiletical theology on God's promises would not just be abstract academic reflection, it would communicate an experience of the joy and beauty of those promises, as is found not least in many of the Psalms and parables. Organic growth implies continuity with the promises of the past. A homiletical theology of promise rooted in poetics would not necessarily conform predetermined notions of an academic essay but would have its own forms and sub-forms, along with principles governing them. Davis speaks about the roots of a sermon deep in Scripture, and the tree

---

40. Walther, *Proper Distinction Between Law and Gospel*, 23, 39.

41. See Jeter, "A Development of Poetic Preaching," 5–12.

42. Bushnell, "Our Gospel, a Gift to the Imagination," 95–117.

43. See, for instance, "The Pharisee and the Publican," in Frederick W. Robertson, *Sermons*, Fifth Series, 36–42.

44. Davis, *Design for Preaching*, 15–16.

showing only leaves and growth natural to its own inner life. He may have had Augustine in the back of his mind when he describes how a sermon should be like an orange tree with fruit for nourishment (i.e., to teach); with flowers offering the hope and joy of harvest, as he says, "for delight"; and growing in warm soil enriched by death, love, trust, and pity (i.e., to move or persuade). Thus, homiletical theology would do what a sermon should do, communicate the character and nature of God in captivating, relational, and inviting ways.

The argument here is that academic homiletical theologians might pay attention to the counsel they have often given the pulpit about poetics in the last fifty years. They would take aesthetic concerns seriously, for instance giving themselves more permission to use metaphor, images, and narratives. They would not limit themselves to the deductive, nor necessarily seek to conform to (or avoid) predetermined notions of what is academic, nor devote themselves primarily to cognitive ways of learning and teaching. Teach, delight and persuade could be bywords of their own craft.

A Concern for Rhetoric

The second area to which we may look for difference in our two kinds of homiletical theology is rhetoric. Aristotle understood rhetoric to provide strategies for the art of persuasion, needed in the Greek *polis* to defend oneself in the court of one's peers. Paul claimed to know nothing about rhetoric (1 Cor 2:1–5) though his speech displayed its use. Augustine refused to instruct his preaching students in rhetoric though it was his former teaching subject,[45] telling them they would learn it by studying and imitating the forms of speech used in the Bible.[46] Whether one knows of rhetoric or not, rhetorical principles are in the culture and influence nearly every act of communication, including preaching.

Classical rhetoric largely fell out of favor by the early 1900s. The rise of public education in the 1800s meant that education had to change: no longer was it based in classical rhetoric, imitating ancient speeches, with oral examinations. Written examinations became standard to handle the large numbers of students. At the same time, the English language went through a period of democratization, and the words and speech patterns of common people became acceptable in education.[47] In the last fifty years, rhetoric has again

---

45. Augustine, *On Christian Doctrine*, 118 (4.1.2).
46. Ibid., 119–120 (4.3.4–4.4.6).
47. Cmiel, *Democratic Eloquence*, 1990.

gained favor: books are again written on rhetoric for preaching,[48] book titles refer to sacred rhetoric,[49] and other volumes hold up the rhetorical effect of biblical texts as models for sermons.[50] The Academy of Homiletics has long had a rhetoric subsection.

In any homiletic, rhetoric is always an issue, acknowledged or not. This is true for homiletical theology that largely conforms to established academic ways of persuasion and identification. It is also true of the more poetic forms of homiletical theology, although different rules apply.

Perhaps nothing points to the renewed influence of rhetoric on preaching so much as the turn to the listener in the New Homiletic. Listeners are not passive recipients of information judged by the preacher to be important for them. They bring their own needs to the sermon—emotional, social, material, spiritual, intellectual—and sermons do not exist merely to make convincing arguments or prove points. Preaching, along with the wider culture, shifted to value communication that anticipates listeners' concerns, allows for pluralism and differences of opinion, encourages diversity, and appreciates that what passes for objectivity is often relative or culturally conditioned. Differences matter. Particularities are important. Preachers strategize to get listeners to identify with what is said. Preachers often try to offer listeners an experience of the Bible and its truth.

Three modes of classical appeal were re-appropriated in recent decades: logos (logic), pathos (emotion), and ethos (the character of the speaker as it is perceived by the listener on any particular topic). Fred B. Craddock developed the idea of an inductive sermon that mirrors the preacher's own inductive journey of discovery with the Bible text through the week.[51] Various sermon forms were advocated, not just deductive, each with its place, some of them hybrid, and each with its downfalls.[52]

Just as H. Grady Davis's poem stands as a marker for new appreciation of poetics in preaching, so too, David James Randolph's proposals for the renewal of preaching back in 1969 can be seen to have anticipated the rhetorical shift that marked the New Homiletic (he was also the first to use the idea of a "new homiletic"). His principles are suggestive for a homiletical theology of promise:

---

48. See for instance, Hogan and Reid, *Connecting with the Congregation*, and Loscalzo, *Preaching Sermons That Connect*.

49. See for instance: Cannon, *Teaching Preaching*, and Pasquarello, *Sacred Rhetoric*.

50. See Long, *Preaching and the Literary Forms of the Bible*, and Graves, *The Sermon as Symphony*.

51. Craddock, *As One Without Authority*.

52. See for instance, Allen, *Patterns of Preaching*.

1) The sermon deals with a *concern* to be shared rather than with a topic to be explained. The sermon proceeds from the Bible as God's Word to us and connects with the situation of the hearers; it does not arise from religion in general to address the universe.

2) The sermon moves fundamentally to *confirmation* from affirmation, rather than to evidence from axiom.

3) The sermon seeks *concretion* by bringing the meaning of the text to expression in the situation of the hearers, rather than abstraction by merely exhibiting the text against its own background.

4) The sermon seeks forms of *construction* and *communication* which are consistent with the message it intends to convey, not necessarily those which are most traditional, most readily available, or most "successful."[53]

Preaching in this view is specific and contextual, not universal and applying to all people the same way, regardless of culture or background. It arises out of needs and interests, "a *concern* to be raised," not a subject for instruction that the speaker determines is important, independent of the listeners. This represents a large rhetorical shift in preaching, not to whatever the listener wants, but to identifying and meeting the actual needs that listeners bring with them to the service. God's promises encounter listeners with saving grace in the precise circumstances of their lives, not primarily in general principles. This encounter is portrayed in the sermon using stories and images specific to the cultures and situations of hearers. A goal is to make biblical stories come to life in the here and now. Randolph anticipated that the form of a biblical promise has a bearing on the shape and message of the sermon.

David Randolph in 1969 was the first person to link preaching and the New Hermeneutic (1964),[54] for which the concept of the language-event or Word-event is central. Language is key. J. L. Austin had already argued that words do things by performing actions like promising, affirming, forgiving, and dreaming.[55] The New Hermeneutic claimed it is impossible to avoid interpretation of Scripture. Moreover, the Word is living, and what God says actually happens (e.g., Gen 1; Isa 55:11). God comes to listeners in and through the words of Scripture as they are read, interpreted, and proclaimed in our time, and things change because of that encounter.[56]

---

53. Randolph, *Renewal of Preaching*, 22–23.
54. Robinson, *The New Hermeneutic*, 1964.
55. In 1955, Austin gave the lectures which became *How to Do Things with Words*, 1962.
56. For an overview of the New Hermeneutic, see Thiselton, "The New Hermeneutic,"

Both to the sermon and some forms of homiletical theology might lay claim to a rhetoric of promise. The latter is inherently performative in at least three ways. First, as James F. Kay says, "a promise is indeed a 'speech act.' A promise, we are told, 'initiates' and 'determines' history; a promise 'binds' its hearers to the future; and a promise 'gives' its receivers a sense of history (and destiny and hope) by 'creating an interval of tension' between its uttering and its redeeming. The performative power . . . is clearly one of agency."[57] In this view, preaching is more than reciting God's speech acts in the past, it is God reiterating those same promises in the present. The experience of agency is the experience of the Agent ("Whoever listens to you listens to me" Luke 10:16). In the preaching of the gospel, and in the power of the Spirit, Christ is encountered and life is changed. The event is both performative and transformative.

Second, Christian language about the future performs that future in the now. A sign only points to its referent but a symbol participates in the reality it represents. Our language for the eschaton is symbolic, yet it is also descriptive and has content and participates in that future. David Buttrick said sermon language gives shape to consciousness.[58] Reinhold Niebhur cautioned that finitude prevents us from describing "the furniture of heaven or the temperature of hell" yet he said that restraint concerning God's promises should not lead "to uncertainty about the validity of hope that 'when he shall appear, we shall be like him; for we shall see him as he is' (1 John 3:2)."[59] Jürgen Moltmann noted that the nature of Christian hope does not limit it to the future: "Does this hope cheat man of the happiness of the present? How could it do so! For it is itself the happiness of the present."[60] James F. Kay notes, "The resurrection becomes saving when it is understood not simply on the literal plane as something that happened to Jesus, but as the symbol for the performative power of the proclaimed gospel awakening the rise of faith in the believer."[61] One might even extend that performative power to ethics. As Augustine once said, "Love all men, even your enemies: love them, not because they are your brothers, but that they may also become your brothers."[62]

308–33.

57. Kay, 121–22. He makes these comments in relation to Jürgen Moltmann on promise.

58. Buttrick, *Homiletic*, 294.

59. Niebuhr, *Nature and Destiny of Man*, Vol. 2, 294.

60. Moltmann, *Theology of Hope*, 32.

61. Ibid., 43.

62. Augustine, *Treatises on the First Letter of John 10:7* (*Patrologia latina* 35, 2059). Cited in Burghardt, *Preaching the Just Word*, 32.

A third dimension of the performative language of promise is proclamation, understood not as a synonym for preaching but as a subset of it. Proclamation participates in God's promissory actions now. Words of testimony to the central good news of the Christ event through faith become resurrection words. The Spirit uses them to give new life to the listeners, with words like, "I will not remember your sins," (Isa 43:25) and "I am with you always," (Matt 25:28). Words of declaration and proclamation, when heard as spoken by one of the Persons of the Trinity today, liberate and comfort. Even less obvious texts can function in this way, like, "a bruised reed [I] will not break, and a dimly burning wick [I] will not quench, [I] will faithfully bring forth justice," (Isa 42:3). To the believer they offer an experience of Christ.

CONCLUSION

We have claimed the need to extend homiletical theology beyond the typical association of it with "academic" or essay-like form and content. We have done so using the subject of promise as a test case. Both academic and poetic expressions of homiletical theology are rooted in the Scripture and tradition, in the promises of the Bible and in constructive or systematic theology and ethics. The academic is propositional and theoretical. The other departs from the first in being attentive to key aspects of poetics and rhetoric that have shaped the New Homiletic. It embodies the principles homiletics advocates for the pulpit. In other words, it does not just talk about promise, it becomes promise-giving and hopeful. It is not the opposite of academic, in fact it might contest the narrowness of what we call academic. At the same time, it is not exclusively concerned with putting scholars in conversation with one another. Nor is it what some people call popular or others dismiss as "dumbing down." It is homiletical, yet it may be readily understood by laypeople. It is written mainly to support preachers and their work in the pulpit, and at times it even models for them what they might do. It concerns itself with information and communication; proposition, image, poetry, and narrative; persuasion and identification; the material, emotional, and spiritual; and with ethos, pathos, and logos. Most important, it is focused not just on reporting the gospel, or giving an account of faith, but in communicating a relationship with the living God who is the future present. In this it may be sacramental, like preaching.

This kind of homiletical theology already exists. There are moments when most homileticians write it, but it is largely unacknowledged as a genre in itself. We may have composed it when asked to give a lecture to a congregation, and we have given something sermonic. It might look like parts of Fredrick Buechner, *Telling the Truth: The Gospel as Tragedy, Comedy and*

Toward a Homiletical Theology of Promise

Fairy Tale;[63] Barbara Brown Taylor, *The Preaching Life;*[64] Katie Geneva Cannon, *Teaching Preaching: Isaac Rufus Clark and Black Sacred Rhetoric;*[65] Fred B. Craddock, *Craddock on the Craft of Preaching;*[66] or Jo Page, *Preaching in My Yes Dress: Confessions of a Reluctant Pastor.*[67]

As I see it, this poetic homiletical theology of promise, in its potential range of hybrid forms, would at times be a kind of poetry that communicates the beauty and mystery of God, in all aspects of God's saving and sustaining ways, together with both the dissonance and coherence of faith. At times, it would communicate the awesome saving power of God, as in the calving of glaciers, where a vast section of ice the size of city blocks, breaks away from the face of a glacier and falls into the sea in seeming slow motion, pushing out a wall of water as it plunges beneath the surface, only to reappear. Or at times it might communicate the beauty of God, as in the fluid flight of a flock of starlings moving as one, the entire flock changing shape and direction with balletic precision in the movement known as murmuration. At times, it would lead to the kind of encounter the disciples had at Emmaus in the breaking of the bread and their eyes being opened.

---

63. Buechner, *Telling the Truth*, 1977.
64. Taylor, *The Preaching Life*, 1993.
65. Katie Geneva Cannon, *Teaching Preaching*, 2002.
66. Craddock, *Craddock on the Craft of Preaching*, 2011.
67. Page, *Preaching in My Yes Dress*, 2016.

—5—

Promissory Kerygmatics

—James F. Kay

"We enjoy Christ only as we embrace Christ clad in his own promises."
JOHN CALVIN

Those who imagine homiletics as an academic discipline where theology and preaching continually and reciprocally rendezvous can only welcome the call for theological reflection on the purpose of preaching in relation to what David Schnasa Jacobsen has termed, "some core sense of the gospel in relation to context."[1] Indeed, "some core sense of the gospel" and some understanding of "context" have been at the heart of both traditional and more radical construals of the Christian message. They have led to a variety of proposals for relating the "core" and the "context" over the course of the Christian movement. Some of these proposals have come from individual theologians, and some have achieved official status by way of conciliar decisions taken by the churches through the centuries. This history prompts a necessary modesty in essaying the case for "promissory kerygmatics."[2]

---

1. David Jacobsen, January 21, 2016, email message to author.
2. I am grateful to the other contributors to this volume, and especially Kenyatta R. Gilbert and David Schnasa Jacobsen, for their comments on an earlier draft of this chapter.

Toward a Homiletical Theology of Promise

FROM HOMILETICS TO KERGYMATICS

The German noun *Homiletik* coined between 1672 and 1675,[3] entered academic parlance as a neologism originally and ultimately derived from the Greek nouns *homilia,* which means communication (See 1 Cor 15:33, KJV) but has also been rendered as company, and *homilos* meaning company or crowd. The latter, in its Lucan verbal forms from *homileo* (cf. Lk 24:14, 15; Acts 20:11; 24:26), refers to conversing, talking with, or discoursing. When *homilia* was transliterated from Greek into ecclesiastical Latin, it regularly referred to the homily, originally as scriptural commentary in the liturgical assembly, but later and more broadly as *sermonic* communication. Note here the formal and relatively neutral meaning of *Homiletik.* While connoting an ecclesiastical context, the term does not indicate the material content of the conversation, communication, or discourse. We also see here a parallel with *Rhetorik,* the subject matter of which can apply to the forms and methods of conversation, communication, or discourse without necessarily touching on their material content, except in relation to the pragmatic goal of successful persuasion. Indeed, the Enlightenment thoroughly recast reflection on preaching within a rhetorical frame of reference. This is seen for example in Johannes Quenstedt's (1617–1688) *Theologia didacto polemica* (1685). He assigns what he terms, "homiletical theology" to "the method of public speaking and the practice of preachers," in short, to rhetoric.[4] Similarly, to recall the definition of another Lutheran theologian, Johann Lorenz von Mosheim (1693–1755), a sermon is not regarded in the first instance with reference to the Word of God, but, rather, *"Eine Predigt ist eine Rede,"* "A sermon is a speech."[5] Reflecting this rhetorical turn in homiletics, Hugh Blair (1718–1800) of Edinburgh declares from his Regius Chair of Rhetoric and Belles-Lettres near his pulpit in St. Giles that "every sermon ... should be a persuasive oration."[6] This is not to say that homiletics as a species of rhetoric was uninterested in theology or Christian doctrine. Such provided the topics for "pulpit eloquence," but theological analysis on the event of preaching itself including theological justification for the use of rhetoric was not integral to rhetorically driven homiletics. The homily or sermon was viewed as part and parcel of the packaging and delivery system for Christian teaching. As such, preaching now becomes the exclusive

3. Caspari, "Homiletik," 295–308.

4. Jacobsen, "What is Homiletical Theology?" 24 citing Lund, *Documents from the History of Lutheranism,* 1517–1750, 222.

5. Mosheim, *Anweisung erbaulich zu predigen,* 1, cited by Josuttis, *Rhetorik und Theologie in der Predigtarbeit,* 9. Karl Barth accepts this definition of Mosheim, only if understood dialectically in relation to preaching as also Word of God. See Barth, *Homiletik,* 99.

6. Blair, *Lectures on Rhetoric and Belles Lettres,* 282.

domain of rhetoric with its contextual concerns for audience and occasion in the service of persuasion. In this particular patterning of "gospel-in-context" bequeathed by an enlightened homiletics, the gospel becomes a topic about which a preacher speaks in the interest of persuading listeners to live by it, a theory-to-practice model in which appeals to reason, emotion, and the probity of the speaker are all intentionally deployed.

It is this model of modern reflection on preaching that was overturned in the revolution wrought by the twentieth century's dialectical theologians. As in the sixteenth-century Reformation, there was again emphasis on God, not as a given topic of a sermon, but as the dynamic and primary Speaker or Agent of authentic preaching; on the promissory character of the kerygma as the correlate of faith; on the proclamation of the kerygma as entailing the continuing humanity and historicity of divine revelation as a contemporary event; and, on the priority of a theological frame of reference for faithfully understanding, critically testing, and responsibly undertaking the divinely authorized and utterly human task of preaching. Going behind the Enlightenment to the "speaking God" of the Protestant Reformers, dialectical theologians, preeminently Rudolf Bultmann, reimagined homiletics as "kerygmatics."[7]

When we inquire further about "some core sense of the gospel," with respect to the task of preaching, it is instructive that in the New Testament "gospel" (*euangelion* = "good news") and "kerygma" ("proclamation") are synonymous. Indeed, in the New Testament, and especially in Paul, "kerygma" is virtually interchangeable with the term "gospel."[8] To seek "some core sense" of one is to seek it with respect to the other, and, in either case, to do so with respect to preaching "in relation to context" as the term kerygma suggests by its connotation of a rhetorical situation that includes listeners.[9] Nevertheless, the notion of "core sense," has been operative in the twentieth century in at least

---

7. In using the nominative form "kerygmatics" in relation to Bultmann's theology of preaching, I am drawing on another German neologism, *Keryktik*, coined originally in 1830 by the pietist scholar Rudolf Stier, who consciously offered it as a competing alternative to *Homiletik*. See his *Grundriss einer biblischen Keryktik, oder einer Anweisung, durch das Wort Gottes sich zur Predigtkunst zu bilden*, 1–2.

8. Dodd, *The Apostolic Preaching and Its Developments*, 28. Dodd's lectures were originally given in 1935. Cf. Bultmann, *Theology of the New Testament*, 1951–1955; (hereinafter cited as *TNT*), 1:317–318, where "*kērygma*" is the object of faith (*pistis*) in 1 Cor 1:21; 2:4–5; 15:11, 14, as is "gospel" in 1 Cor 15:2 and Phil 1:27.

9. Karl Barth resists Bultmann's construal of kerygmatic proclamation precisely because it connotes "a summons to human decision," which, in Barth's view, "is in no sense constitutive for the task of preaching." For this reason, Barth substitutes for "proclamation" (*Verkündigung*) or *kērygma* the term "announcement" (*Ankündigung*) or *epangelia* "which does not carry with it a summons to human decision." Barth, *Homiletik*, 32.

two related but ultimately diverging ways. This divergence affects dramatically how preaching should be understood and undertaken.

To concretize matters, recall the pre-Pauline formulation of the gospel that Apostle Paul links directly to his proclamation or kerygma:

> Now I would remind you brothers and sisters, of the gospel [*euangelion* = "good news"] that I proclaimed [*euēngelisamēn* = "gospeled"] to you, which you in turn received, in which also you stand through which also you are being saved if you hold firmly to the message I proclaimed [*euēngelisamēn* = "gospeled"] to you—unless you have come to believe in vain.
>
> For I handed over to you as of first importance what I in turn had received: that Christ died for our sins in accordance with the scriptures, and that he was buried, and that he was raised on the third day in accordance with the scriptures, and that he appeared to Cephas, then to the twelve . . . (1 Cor 15:1–5)

Paul goes on to declare to the Corinthian congregation, "If Christ has not been raised, then our proclamation [*kērygma*] has been in vain and your faith has been in vain" (1 Cor 15:14). Thus, for Paul the death and resurrection of Jesus Christ are central to the gospel and the apostolic kerygma.[10] Moreover, the noun "kerygma" can refer either to the *content* of what is proclaimed (1 Cor 15:4) or to the *act* of proclaiming it (1 Cor 2:4).[11] This distinction is key to two competing "core senses" potentially informing "kerygmatics," one oriented to fixed doctrinal content about Jesus Christ; the other to the contemporary event of Jesus Christ.

THE CORE SENSE OF THE KERYGMA: FIXED CONTENT

Among the senses in which the content of the apostolic kerygma has been taken as core is as a "rule of faith." For example, C. H. Dodd offers a synthetic reconstruction of the Christian kerygma from its pre-Pauline stage through Paul, Acts, the Synoptics, and John to find and to fuse together their common elements. He regards these elements as historical "*data* of the Christian faith," whose "content . . . entered into the Rule of Faith, which is recognized

---

10. We find similarly compressed kerygmatic kernels or summaries sprinkled throughout Paul's undisputed letters (e.g., Rom 4:25; 6:10; 8:34; 10:9; 14:9; 2 Cor 5:15; 13:4; and, 1 Thess 4:14), in addition to the pre-Pauline material cited above from 1 Cor 15:3–5 and the "Christ hymn" embedded in Phil 2:5–11.

11. See *Theological Dictionary of the New Testament* (hereinafter cited as *TDNT*), s.v. "*kēryx* [etc.]."

by the theologians of the second and third centuries as the presupposition of Christian theology. Out of the Rule of Faith in turn the Creeds emerged. The so-called Apostles' Creed in particular still betrays in its form and language its direct descent from the primitive apostolic Preaching."[12] In Dodd's view, the "core sense of the gospel" is retrievable from the New Testament itself as creedal bullet points, a *fides quae*, awaiting contemporary interpretation. Since Dodd regards the reconstructed original kerygma as consisting of truth claims requiring cognitive assent, he is not unaware that preachers today still have to engage questions as to their truth and relevance.[13] When the "core sense" of the kerygma is thus taken as its original *content*, it functions as a perdurably fixed, foundational "deposit of faith" (*fidei depositum*) upon which to draw when proclaiming the gospel into a particular context. In other words, the kerygma is primarily understood as something that can be taken "in hand" by way of *ressourcement*, and the church transmits or reproduces it either by means of the Magisterium (as in Roman Catholicism) or by exegetical brilliance or homiletical prowess (as in much Protestantism). Nevertheless, in his self-confined role as an academic historian of early Christianity, Dodd is relatively reticent about how these petrified stones might become living bread for proclamation today.

This interpretation of the kerygma's "core sense of the gospel," however, was and continues to be challenged today by the New Testament theology of Rudolf Bultmann. While centering his theology on a historical retrieval of the kerygma, Bultmann took the meaning of its core sense in a different direction from that of a permanently formulated "rule of faith" to be delivered by contemporary pulpit discourse. Rather, the "core sense of the gospel" in terms of the kerygma is not found in its alleged invariable or univocal *content* throughout history, rather it is found in its paradoxical character as God's continuing "eschatological *event*" in history.

THE CORE SENSE OF THE KERGYMA: THE ESCHATOLOGICAL EVENT OF JESUS CHRIST

The noun *kērygma* admittedly appears only nine times in the New Testament and only four times in the undisputed Pauline letters, but these appearances "indicate a connection between proclamation, revelation, and salvation in early Christianity."[14] This is seen, for example, in 1 Cor 1:21, "For since, in the

---

12. Dodd, *The Apostolic Preaching and Its Developments*, 14, 73–74.
13. Ibid., 76–78.
14. Congdon, *Rudolf Bultmann*, 63, and noting Rom 16:25–26a; 1 Cor 1:21; 2:4–5;

wisdom of God, the world did not know God through wisdom, God decided, through the foolishness of our proclamation [*kērygma*], to save those who believe." Thus, the "kerygma or proclamation is the vehicle of God's saving power, the human word through which God's word of revelation confronts us."[15] Moreover, the kerygma's theological and Christological claims are always simultaneously proclaimed as anthropological and soteriological ones. The destiny of Jesus is thus intertwined with the destiny of those to whom the news of his destiny is addressed. As Ricoeur notes, Paul "invites the hearer of the word to decipher the movement of his own existence in the light of the Passion and Resurrection of Christ. Hence, the death of the old man and the birth of the new creature are understood under the sign of the Cross and the Paschal victory."[16] For one to say, "Jesus is Lord," is simultaneously to confess that, "I am his subject," an acknowledgement of a relational or personal bond with this Lord that is understood as saving. Whereas Dodd identifies the "core sense of the gospel" with its traditional content, Bultmann identifies it with its continuing existential eventfulness as God's speaking efficaciously into the lives of particular hearers. For this reason, Bultmann generally uses the term "kerygma" rather than "gospel" precisely to accent the gospel's core sense as the contemporary divine event of revelation and salvation by way of God's personal, direct address mediated to its hearers through human speech.

While the apostolic kerygma admittedly proclaims what first-century Christians likely regarded as "facts" about the destiny of Jesus as the crucified and risen Lord or Christ, nevertheless, "the word of proclamation is no mere report about historical incidents" or "teaching . . . which could simply be regarded as true without any transformation of the hearer's own existence. For the word is kerygma, personal address [*Anrede*], demand [*Forderung*], and promise [*Verheissung*]; it is the very act of divine grace."[17] Here, Bultmann imagines proclaimers of the gospel on analogy with that of dispatched heralds or envoys [*kērykes*; *apostoloi*] running ahead of a royal entourage to proclaim the news of the monarch's imminent arrival. "So we are ambassadors for Christ," Paul writes, "God making his appeal through us" (2 Cor 5:20). When human proclamation is heard as God word (1 Thess 2:13), it is as a summoning message directed to the listener's conscience (*syneidesis*, 2 Cor

---

and, 15:14.

15. Ibid., 63.

16. Ricoeur, "Preface to Bultmann," 52.

17. *TNT*, 1:319. Cf. Rudolf Bultmann, *Theologie des Neuen Testaments*, 9th ed., ed. Otto Merk (Tübingen: J. C. B. Mohr [Paul Siebeck], 1984; hereinafter cited as *TdNT*), 319. See also Bultmann, *TNT*, 1:302; and cf. Bultmann, *TdNT*, 301, where the proclaimed word is characterized as "*anredenden, fordernden und verheissenden.*"

4:2, 5:11; cf. Rom 2:15). It declares the promise of salvation not as information to be assessed but as personal transformation to be embraced.[18]

Thus, from Bultmann's standpoint, what is definitively fixed as kerygma, and is key to its continuing interpretation amid a variety of shifting circumstances, is the personal bond between God and humanity established in and through the contemporary proclamation of and by Jesus Christ.[19] This is arguably the core sense or *Sache* (subject matter) of the *kerygma*: its material revelatory power is neither exhausted by nor confined to its *Sprache* or linguistic formulations, however ancient or however official.

> *Theological propositions*—even those of the New Testament—can never be the *object* of faith; they can only be the explication of the understanding which is inherent in faith itself. Being such explications, they are determined by the believer's situation and are necessarily incomplete. This *incompleteness*, however, is not a lack to be remedied by future generations . . . Rather, the incompleteness has its cause in the inexhaustibility of believing comprehension, which must ever actualize itself anew; this incompleteness consequently signifies a task and a promise.[20]

That is to say, given the saving relationship between God and humanity enacted and embodied through Christian proclamation, any received formulations of the kerygma, as artifacts or "remains of the day" from previous iterations, can never simply be recycled as a final human word eternally frozen in time. Rather, to exchange metaphors of solidity for those of liquidity, the kerygma always runs fluently and fluidly from the eschatological future of Jesus Christ toward the historical present thereby melting the permafrost of fixed understandings about what "cross-resurrection" or "Jesus Christ" might

---

18. On conscience and proclamation in Paul, see Bultmann, 1:*TNT*, 1:218, 250, and 260–261. This formal pattern of proclamation as demand and promise is also typical of the preaching of Jesus and the prophets before him. But what separates the kerygma of Paul and the apostles from that of Jesus is that the church proclaims Jesus' eschatological destiny as decisive for salvation. In Bultmann's celebrated catchphrase, "The proclaimer became the proclaimed." Bultmann, *TNT*, 1:33.

19. "Der Verkündigte zugleich als der Verkünder präsent ist." Rudolf Bultmann, "*Allgemeine Wahrheiten und christliche Verkündingung* [1957]," 3:169. Statements such as this are based on Bultmann's exegesis of Paul that uncovers double patterns of predication. The same soteriological benefits attributed to the death and resurrection of Christ are also attributed by Paul to the proclamation and proclaimers (as proclaimers) of the kerygma. For a compendium of Pauline examples, see Kay, *Christus Praesens*, 49–58.

20. Bultmann, *TNT*, 2:237–38: Here is one source of that freedom Bultmann bequeathed to his students such as Gerhard Ebeling and Ernst Fuchs with their "post-Bultmannian" counterproposals offering fresh explications of the kerygma in relation to "the historical Jesus."

actually mean "under the compulsion of a concrete situation."[21] Hermeneutically, the human responsibility for intelligible address also precludes the identification of a textual starting block with the communicative finish line thereby nullifying the eventful "run" of the proclamation itself. Precluded as well is mouthing the kerygma's scriptural code words in the predictable manner of "chancel-speak" or "preacher talk," what Kenyatta Gilbert has elsewhere termed "parrot theology," a danger to which even some of Bultmann's followers have not been immune.[22] If the formulations of the kerygma are to become existentially relevant to the concrete situation of the listeners, then preaching must not only honor the concerns of rhetoric for audience and occasion, and Bultmann's concern for hermeneutical intentionality in textual interpretation and translation, *but the promised in-breaking of God's saving Word in and through the event of human communication.*[23] "Kerygma" thus entails utterly human and utterly vital rhetorical and hermeneutical responsibilities for the church of the Word. These responsibilities are undertaken within a posture of prayer awaiting God's next move promised through the continuing eschatological mission of the earthly Jesus as the *Christus praesens* ("Christ who is present"), the acting Agent of the kerygma's saving proclamation.

KERYGMA AND DOGMA

Given the reformulation by Bultmann of the "core sense" of the kerygmatic gospel, what role should the formulations of the kerygma found in the New Testament continue to play in the church's mission and preaching? First of all, these formulations, including those "handed over" to Paul (e.g., 1 Cor 15:1–3; Phil 2:5–11), are themselves theological reflections and constructions that employ and reflect the operative world pictures (*Weltbilder*) of their time and place, those historically conditioned or time-bound assumptions distinct from our own, what the American historian, Carl Becker, once called "climates of opinion."[24] The implication that follows is that historians, and we

---

21. Bultmann, *TNT*, 1:190.

22. See Dorothee Sölle's *Political Theology*, 23, where she accuses Walther Schmithals of suppressing Bultmann's distinction between "kerygma" and "dogma," thereby collapsing the kerygmatic event into invariable dogmas unrelated to the contemporary situation into which they are spoken.

23. Without seeking to minimize possible differences, Kenyatta Gilbert's formulation of prophetic preaching as "God-summoned speech clothed in cultural particularity" nicely captures Bultmann's view of kerygmatic proclamation. Cf. Gilbert, *A Pursued Justice*, 6.

24. Becker, *The Heavenly City of the Eighteenth-Century Philosophers*, 1–31. Becker acknowledges Alfred North Whitehead in retrieving this seventeenth-century term.

might add, theologians or preachers, too, are themselves operating within their own specific cultural *Weltbilder* and are, therefore, inevitably bandying about commonplaces that are part and parcel of their contemporary intellectual and cultural scene—just as others did who went before them and who will follow after them.

As a historian trained in the methods of the *Religionsgeschichtliche Schule*, Bultmann completely accepts this radically contingent character of all conceptual frameworks. The logic of this position relativizes Bultmann's own knowledge and interpretation of the past history of the kerygma; and, with each decade we see more clearly how Bultmann's theology is both a witness to his believing self-understanding in the light of Jesus Christ while simultaneously reflecting a historical moment governed by the climates of opinion and plausibility structures of his own twentieth-century German context, and which often go by the shorthand of "modernity." Similarly, we, too, cannot escape our own "social locations" as we respond to the God of the gospel in the continuing human tasks of thinking about this God, and engaging in the kinds of historical reconstruction, literary analysis, and attention to rhetoric that are ingredients to intelligible scriptural interpretation and preaching. If Bultmann's now dated historiography arguably betrays some threads of "anti-Judaism," despite his exemplary conduct toward Jews under the totalitarian conditions of the Third Reich,[25] so those of us in the United States who are ethnically white have to consider the ways in which our own readings and interpretations of the kerygma may themselves be captive to the pervasive cultural climate of "whiteness" skewing our discourse and Christian witness despite our intentions.[26]

Nevertheless, Bultmann values the historically received traditional formulations of the saving significance of Jesus Christ, however wrapped in the conceptuality or cosmology of the first century, whether derived from Hellenized Second Temple Judaism, or (and this would be historically disputed today) incipient Gnosticism. Why? Because such borrowed and adapted concepts (e.g., "Messiah," "resurrection," "end of the Age," "blood atonement," etc.) give us a window into the believing self-understanding emerging in the initial decades of the church's life, and, thereby provide a record of human response to divine revelation that shows interpretive freedom amid a variety of historical circumstances. But in contrast to characterizations of Christian faith by both fundamentalists and many secularists, believing today in Jesus Christ as Lord does not mean believing everything in the Bible, including ancient

---

25. For a judicious appraisal of Bultmann on this question, see Standhartinger, "Bultmann's Theology of the New Testament in Context," 233-55.

26 26 See Jensen, *The Heart of Whiteness*.

understandings of the cosmos. Moreover, the kerygmatic confessions even of Paul's gospel are not revelation, are not in their own power God's living Word or Jesus Christ; they are rather "dogmas" that humanly witness to the event of God's living Word or Jesus Christ at a particular moment in time and place. These kerygmatic formulations, while not identifiable in a 1:1 correspondence to revelation, may subsequently and indirectly serve contemporary kerygmatic proclamation as a starting point for sermonic exposition or theological reflection, and by the variety of their interpretive moves authorize our own.[27]

Certainly, the methods of historical science problematize superficial readings of both the kerygmatic formulations of the church found in its scriptures as well as the task of contemporary proclamation. (This is probably self-evident to homiletics professors!) But the distinction between historical content and eschatological event, between God's self-actualizing Word in Jesus Christ and the human word of witness to it, bestows on theological work and preaching not only a freedom from the burden of playing God but also a reverence for the otherness of God and a respect for witnesses of the gospel other than ourselves, both past and present, who have risked and still risk pointing to where God is acting and speaking. In light of this continuing witness to God's continuing revelation, we cannot assume that we definitively possess the kerygma as such simply because we recite the Apostles' Creed or have memorized scriptural, catechetical, or liturgical texts. As Bultmann writes,

> It is becoming increasingly apparent to me that the central problem of New Testament theology is to say what the Christian kerygma actually is. It is never present simply as something given, but is always formulated out of a particular believing understanding . . . What the kerygma is can never be said conclusively, but must constantly be found anew, because it is only actually the kerygma in the carrying out of the proclamation.[28]

This means that while Christian preaching always takes account of traditional kerygmatic formulations, we cannot assume in advance or a priori what

---

27. Bultmann, *TNT*, 1:318.

28. Congdon, *Bultmann*, 71, quoting and translating from Bultmann and Heidegger, *Briefwechsel 1925–1975*, 186. Congdon further observes that Bultmann's "distinction here between kerygma and scripture corresponds to Karl Barth's distinction between revelation and scripture," and "like Barth, Bultmann refuses to collapse kerygma and theology." On this point Barth and Bultmann agree: "The sovereign freedom of God precludes the collapse of revelation as the act of God, into scripture, preaching, or theology as the human witnesses to revelation." Congdon, *Bultmann*, 72. I would add that Bultmann arguably transposes the Chalcedonian definition of the two natures of Jesus Christ into an epistemological axiom as he navigates the distinction-in-relation between the God of the eschaton and the historicity of humanity, "without confusion" but "without separation."

the kerygma as revelation is, or will become, or how it will be heard in relation to "the compulsion of a concrete situation." Why? Because the ultimate preacher of the Word of God is Jesus Christ, amid our humanity and historicity and that of the kerygma's human heralds. In this sense, the kerygma is never "in hand" as our possession; it is ever "at hand" from the eschatological future of Jesus Christ.[29] This does not preclude but sustains our hermeneutical responsibility to "translate" first-century kerygmatic dogmas into the linguistic idioms and diverse cultures of our own time. This preaching task is, of course, highly risk-taking, but the perdurance of the preaching office itself indicates that the meaning of the kerygma for any concrete situation *is never obvious* or simply conveyed by narrative recital. The church, like the synagogue, requires more than scriptural lectors and cantors. It requires preachers. The kerygma demands of us the courage of continuing interpretation and existential translation into ever new, even unforeseen situations, a responsibility that can only be undertaken by trusting in the continuing paracletic promise and presence of the Spirit of Jesus Christ (John 14:15–17, 25; 15:26–27; 16:12–15).

THE PROMISSORY KERYGMA AND THE CHRISTUS PRAESENS

Because all formulations of the kerygma are temporal and not eternal, even the most responsible interpretations, including those of Bultmann himself, cannot guarantee a correspondence between human speech about God and speech from God. As Bultmann himself notes, "Certainly in the framework of theology, homiletics is necessary as a doctrine of preaching. However, no homiletics can transmit to an individual preacher a method which guarantees to him that his sermon will be genuine proclamation, any more than there can be a church order through which it is guaranteed that the church in any particular historical form achieves its authentic meaning: to be the scene of the eschatological occurrence."[30] So, what transforms the kerygma from mythical narrative, historical information, or doctrinal deposit *about* Jesus Christ— that is, mere artifact or even dead letter—into the lively summons *from* Jesus Christ in which are encountered the demand and promise of eschatologically determined existence?

Bultmann's answer is that, "Only Christ can give the kerygmatic character to everything which is 'taught' as Christian. It is only Christ who transfigures the doctrine into kerygma. Therefore, Christ is correctly preached not

---

29. Cf. Morse, *The Difference Heaven Makes*, 6–7, 122.
30. Bultmann, "Reply," 277.

where something is said *about* him, but only where he himself becomes the proclaimer."³¹ Thus, the resurrection or revelation of Jesus Christ is no longer regarded by Bultmann as a mythical-historical event of the past on the basis of which Christian witness becomes efficacious by its accurate iteration or portrayal of this past event. Rather, for Bultmann, the divinely given efficacy of Christian witness in history *is* the resurrection or revelation of Jesus Christ.

Given the personal or existential bond established in the eschatological event of proclamation, can we say anything more that might illumine its contours without trespassing on God's freedom, while giving some account of how divine revelation is heard through understandable words of address rather than simply the invocations of dogmas of the past? To begin, Bultmann operates with an "I-Thou" model or analogy of revelation as entailing existential commitments. Specifically, he construes the presence of Christ to an individual as analogous to the encounter of a Lover and a Beloved when and where the former says to the latter, "I love you." The statement, "I love you," is arguably a promise and simultaneously an existential statement in that it does not simply convey information but a self-involving declaration. In saying, "I love you," the speaker does not discourse *about* love but *enacts* love concretely. This word of love is the love of which it speaks.³²

Earlier I noted Bultmann's description of the proclaimed kerygma as "personal address [*Anrede*], demand [*Forderung*], and promise [*Verheissung*]; it is the very act of divine grace." The theme of promise is admittedly more assumed than developed by Bultmann, but his discussions of existential language suggest its potential connections with the discussions of Anglo-American analytic philosophy on such topics as "performative utterance" and "commissive self-involvement."³³ To acknowledge the kerygma as a promise is to say, in analytic terms, that it commits the speaker to doing something either by assuming an obligation or declaring an intention, what J. L. Austin calls a "commissive." Words heard with commissive force "self involve" an agent or subject as Donald Evans once argued. When we hear the kerygma with

---

31. Bultmann, "Introduction," xvi. Bultmann therefore accepts the formulation of Eduard Ellwein that "Jesus has risen in the kerygma" provided "it expresses the fact that Jesus is really present in the kerygma; that it is *his* word which involves the hearer in the kerygma." Bultmann, "The Primitive Christian Kerygma and the Historical Jesus," in *The Historical Jesus and the Kerygmatic Christ*, 42, Cf. 30.

32. See Bultmann, *Jesus Christ and Mythology*, 75–76. Hence, faith in the kerygma simultaneously entails for Paul what Bultmann calls, "a personal relationship to Christ" (citing Rom 6:8; 10:9, 14; Gal 2:20; and Phlm 5). See *TDNT*, s.v. "*pisteuō* [etc.]."

33. See Austin, "Performative Utterances [1956]," 220–39; Austin, *How to Do Things with Words*, esp. 150–151 and 162; and Evans, *The Logic of Self-Involvement*, 32, 158, and 164–165.

"commissive force," as a promise directed to us, such force necessarily entails the Promissor's self-involvement and simultaneously calls for our correlative response of faith in the promise. Since a promise always entails its promisor, when the kerygma is heard as a promise *of* Christ, then it is heard in faith as a promise *from* Christ himself (Rom 10:17; 2 Cor 5:20, 13:3). Thus, the *Christus praesens* is logically entailed by the promissory character of his word. Moreover, heard as a promise, "I love you," also functions as a demand, insofar as it places the Addressee in a new situation, namely, of being the Beloved, which requires a response, whether positive or negative, that is determinative for the Addressee's self-understanding.

Here, some qualifications on the role of linguistic analysis in relation to the theological deployment of promise are warranted. First of all, while appeals to analytic philosophy may have apologetic resonance, no linguistic analysis can demonstrate independently of faith's response that the Lover promising eternal fidelity is in fact the Christ of God, but linguistic analysis does suggest that the ordinary usage of the language of promise is a fitting medium for divine communication. Second, many of the New Testament's formulations of the kerygma, including that from 1 Corinthians 15 quoted above, do not satisfy all of the rules that analytic philosophers, such as John Searle, identify as necessary for a promissory speech act to occur.[34] Yet, the believing self-understanding of the faithful through the ages testifies that they are nevertheless received and heard in faith as God's promises. Thus, while divine accommodation to the human linguistic condition pertains to the freedom of God, the election of human language by God, including the language of promise, does not mean that the Christ of God is bound or subject to this medium or its identified conventions in the event of revelation. Thus, the relation between divine and human speech remains one of paradoxical identity, but it is an identity ultimately established by God.[35] Finally, analytic philosophy operates with a very limited notion of extra-linguistic cultural "context" where it deals with it at all. In *Expression and Meaning*, Searle does discuss the role of an "extra-linguistic institution," such as the church, in order for an illocutionary speech act, such as absolution, to be performed.[36] Certainly, one

---

34. Searle, *Speech Acts*, 57–64.

35. While the term "double agency" is now commonly used in speaking of coincident divine and human activity in the event of revelation, Bultmann's term, "paradoxical identity," is arguably preferable in order to encapsulate a non-competitive, simultaneous unity-in-distinction of divine and human agents. See Bultmann, "On the Problem of Demythologizing," 111. For an exposition of "paradoxical identity" occasioned by Karl Barth's discussion of baptism, see McMaken, "Definitive, Defective or Deft? Reassessing Barth's Doctrine of Baptism in *Church Dogmatics* IV/4," 98–107.

36. Searle, *Expression and Meaning*, 7.

can affirm this "extra-linguistic" acknowledgement, but is the personal relationship forged by a promise between the Promisor and the Promisee, and for that matter within any acknowledged "extra-linguistic" institutional context, ever independent or isolatable from its larger embedment in culture? In other words, analytic philosophy privileges the "linguistic" over the "cultural" in relation to context, and for this reason alone *"speech act theory is not a comprehensive philosophy of language"* or *"a solution to the hermeneutical problem."*[37]

THE KERYGMA AND CONTEXT: A REFLECTION ON ESCHATOLOGICAL EXISTENCE

Perhaps no homiletical theology other than Bultmann's has argued more strenuously for the hermeneutical importance of context and simultaneously been more frequently accused of ignoring it entirely. To reintroduce Bultmann into North American homiletical discussion thus requires some accounting of how promissory kerygmatics with its emphasis on the personal relationship between Jesus Christ and the contemporary believer's self-understanding can credibly entail Bultmann's conviction that "it is actually the task of any theology to consider the *responsibility* of faith for the structures of the present world."[38] On the one hand, since the kerygma's theological statements are simultaneously anthropological confessions of believing self-understanding, the eschatological event in history, which is Jesus Christ, is likewise simultaneously encountered in faith as a call to eschatological existence in the maelstroms of history. On the other hand, Bultmann is charged with an understanding of theology and preaching that, in Kenyatta Gilbert's words drawn from a different discussion, seemingly "lacks color, that is, context-specific content." Similarly, Jürgen Moltmann and Dorothee Sölle albeit in different ways, and for trenchant if tendentious reasons, both criticized Bultmann's existentialist construal of salvation as withdrawing his kerygma from any specific engagement with the contemporary social and political context.[39] In transposing the mythological apocalyptic dualism between the present evil age and the messianic age to come into a dualism of decision for or against the scandal of the cross of Jesus Christ and the call to love the neighbor, Bultmann, in concert with the Lutheran tradition understands the Christian life as both "freedom

---

37. Briggs, *Words in Action*, 6 and 12. Italics original.

38. Standhartinger, "Bultmann's Theology of the New Testament in Context," 255, with the quotation from Bultmann taken from Rudolf Bultmann to Dorothee Sölle, August 1971. Bultmann Papers, MS 2-2386, p. 1. University of Tübingen Library.

39. Moltmann, *Theology of Hope*, esp. 45–69; and, Sölle, *Political Theology*, xix, where she claims that Bultmann's theology "understands itself as essentially apolitical."

from" determination by godless powers and "freedom for" the world through obedience to God on behalf of the neighbor in need. Given the totalitarian conditions under which Bultmann's mature theological work came to fruition, amid the harrowing constraints on individual freedom of conscience and expression, the "freedom from" dimension in the dialectic of the Christian life as eschatological existence in history is arguably much more strongly articulated in Bultmann than is any eschatological ethic with programmatic or political specificity.

Given this limitation that seems inherent in Bultmann, one way to move forward may be through kerygmatic *narration*. On the one hand, speech-act theory helps us to move conceptually and plausibly beyond Jesus Christ as a mere inference or reference in proclamation to Jesus Christ as a commissive Referent or acting Subject of an utterance heard in faith as a promise from God. Divine agency in kerygmatic proclamation is thus personal and existential rather than impersonal or mechanistically causal. As a promisor, Jesus Christ includes both a who and a what, that is both self-involvement and commitments that have content. Nevertheless, *while a promise entails a self-involving promisor, it cannot reveal the content of the promisor's character or commitments.* For this reason, we not only need promissory kerygmatics, but we need kerygmatic *narratives* to identify who Jesus was as Lord and Christ and to identify what obedience to him entailed, in order to translate these identity descriptions that are simultaneously artifacts of believing self-understanding into the contemporary context.[40] The Synoptic Gospels, for example, retrospectively edited in light of the destiny of Jesus Christ as crucified and risen, provide this kind of kerygmatic narrative identification, albeit one that is shaped by a first-century world picture awaiting contemporary demythologizing. For this reason, *promissory* kerygmatics reminds both liberals and postliberals that the excessive and mistaken claims for historical or narrative renderings as equivalent to the contemporary reality or real presence of Jesus Christ must be challenged by the recognition that it is the promissory and eschatological character of kerygmatic proclamation through which that presence and resulting freedom for the neighbor is confessed.[41] On the other hand, promissory *kerygmatics* can gain concreteness from the insistence of postliberalism that scriptural narratives furnish meaningful identity descriptions both of Jesus Christ and of the lineaments of the Christian life. Here is where

---

40. I am adapting with a Bultmannian twist the argument of Thiemann, *Revelation and Theology*, esp. 93–94. Cf. Morse's "promissory narration" as proposed in, *The Logic of Promise in Moltmann's Theology*, 106, 116, 131, and taken up homiletically in James F. Kay, *Preaching and Theology*, 105–128.

41. For my criticism of postliberalism on this point, see *Christus Praesens*, 137–42; and, *Preaching and Theology*, 117–20.

the impasse between Bultmann's *Theology of the New Testament* and Dorothee Sölle's "political theology" of "the historical Jesus" might be mutually reviewed and revised in light of more recent theological reflection.

I should like to conclude, however, in a more provocative vein. The question I would like to pose is whether Bultmann's focus on eschatological existence as "freedom from" the world might not prove salutary for a renewed homiletical theology in our present situation. By "freedom from" the world, I mean in so far as that world as a socio-cultural-political power network or "field-force" refuses to recognize its own impertinence and impermanence before the living God. Recent political events in the United States suggest that the call for eschatological existence may once again require a kerygmatic setting free from those cultural patterns and political structures determined to ride roughshod over human dignity and decency. One suggests this response for today's American context at the risk of being heard as either existentially reinforcing our culture's longstanding "rugged individualism," with its libertarian politics and laissez faire economics, or, contrariwise, as departing from our perennial and righteous Puritan impulse to order the agenda of politics and to define specific legislation in light of a "Christian worldview," or "social program," whether in a conservative or liberal vein. Both responses from all sides of the ideological compass would seem confirmed in their rejections of Bultmann's concept of *Entweltlichung*, literally, "deworldlizing," sometimes translated as "desecularizing," to characterize the paradox of eschatological existence that he finds in Paul's words in 1 Cor 7:29–31.

> I mean brothers and sisters, the appointed time has grown short; from now on, let even those who have wives be as though they had none, and those who mourn as though they were not mourning, and those who rejoice as though they were not rejoicing, and those who buy as though they had no possessions, and those who deal with the world as though they had no dealings with it. For the present form of this world is passing away.

In a recent essay, Angela Standhartinger correlates Bultmann's own biography with his writings to show how this very passage from Paul guided his steadfast Christian witness under the totalitarian conditions of the Third Reich. Honoring the eschatological call (*hōs mē*, "as though not") meant for Bultmann, in his context, the withdrawal from a self-assured socio-cultural-political world that did not recognize or acknowledge its impermanence and impertinence before the living God. Guided by this Pauline interpretation of the kerygma for concrete existence, Bultmann in his time stood critically against the prevailing Nazi worldview, with its racism, nationalism, Hitler personality cult, and subordination of individual freedom. Such freedom *from* the world simultaneously enabled a freedom *for* the world manifested in acts of love and justice, which, in Bultmann's case, included his leadership of the Marburg theological faculty in publicly resisting the extension of the Aryan paragraph excluding those of Jewish heritage from ordained office or membership in the church, his counter-cultural hospitality to Jewish colleagues and students under duress, his participation in the Pastors' Emergency League and the Confessing Church, and the opening of his home to refugees at the war's end. Yet in a time when many Protestant preachers in America seemingly talk endlessly of themselves, Standhardinger observes how little Bultmann hints in any of his published writings, and we might add in his sermons, about his own believing existence and acts of witness. Why this reticence?[42]

Commenting on Bultmann's concept of *Entweltlichung*, David W. Congdon writes, "The new self-understanding of faith that corresponds to the kerygmatic word is not at all a solipsistic turning in upon oneself. On the contrary, it is in fact a self-displacement and a self-dispossession in the sense that God's eschatological action in Christ interrupts our bondage to the world and to ourselves and breaks us open to what arrives on the scene from God's future, and thus what meets us in the face of the neighbor and stranger . . . We are estranged *from* the world in order to live for those who have been estranged *by* the world."[43] We see here the dialectic of the cross and resurrection, which are really two sides of one eschatological event, etched into the self-understanding of the Christian. There is a detachment, a putting to death or crucifying of all in us that denies or resists the love of neighbor, and an awakening of our responsibility to embrace a new life determined by love rather than death. In this sense, "the word of the cross" (1 Cor 1:18) is simultaneously the "word of life" (Phil 2:16).

For this reason, and in contrast to the liberation theologies of the 1960s and 1970s, Bultmann did not make the contours of his own personal existence in faith or that of any particular historical context, past or present, the material

---

42. Standhartinger, "Bultmann's Theology of the New Testament in Context," 233–55. See also Hammann, *Rudolf Bultmann*, esp. 267–368, which discusses Bultmann's "time of testing" during the Nazi period.

43. For a comprehensive exposition of *Entweltlichung* in Bultmann's thought, see Congdon, *The Mission of Demythologizing*, 766–87, quoting here from 778. For "an ethics of interruption," see also Zoloth, "Interrupting Your Life," 3–24. Zoloth's views offer parallels with Bultmann's sense of the kerygma as an in-breaking event that transforms one's self-understanding toward a world revealed as unraveling. See Congdon, *The God Who Saves*, 97–98, for his discussion of Zoloth. Rowan Williams also reflects on the "dispossession of Christ's cross" that "is finished only in communicating to human beings of the divine liberty in their fleshly and historical lives—in the shorthand of doctrinal language, the sharing of Jesus' risen life." See Williams, *On Christian Theology*, 12.

subject matter of his theology—whether exegetical or homiletical in genre. This arguably leads characterizations of eschatological existence to a certain, perhaps necessary, lack in "context-specific content." As Standhartinger again observes,

> [T]he kerygma reveals itself in the respective concrete situation of existence, indeed always when one's previous existence becomes questionable, and it reveals itself as the possibility of a new self-understanding. This new self-understanding remains abstract and formalized, however, to the extent that the kerygma contains the (unchanging) call to decision whose respective enactments cannot be explicated because they must remain acts or deeds of concrete life.[44]

This existentialist restraint in refraining from a homiletical theology geared to programmatic ethical imperatives and empirical outcomes arguably reflects the constraints on Christian witness imposed by a totalitarian dictatorship. But only in part. Bultmann also resists definitive foreclosures on "what" the proclaimed kerygma would call any individual to do in the face of God's constantly unfolding future. Here, too, the Christian must walk "by faith and not by sight" (2 Cor 5:7).

This restraint in offering definitive ethical imperatives is notably coupled with a frequent absence of direct ethos and pathos appeals in the service of those imperatives. While this absence may well reflect the constraints of totalitarianism on the "how" of preaching, it also affords a positive countersign. In contrast to the manipulative and deceitful communication norms operative in a propaganda-ridden "post-truth" society, the open and sincere proclamation of the gospel (2 Cor 1:12; 6:11) respects listeners and affords them space to encounter the call of love. Bultmann thereby points his listeners and readers to the eschatological gift of freedom amid enslaving worldly norms to discover and reflect on what may be required of them in their own particular circumstances. Thus, Bultmann's interpretation of the Pauline "as if not" authorizes a kind of apophatic public theology, an example of "internal immigration," that negates, "de-normalizes," or delegitimizes the sovereignty of the presumptuous principalities and powers. Here we see a formalized principle ("as if not") calling for the withdrawal of customary or expected attention, deference, or allegiance, without specifying or prescribing in advance how practices effecting de-legitimation will materially occur.[45] Paradoxically, "Despite or

---

44. Standhartinger, "Bultmann's Theology of the New Testament in Context," 249.

45. For an example of the positive role of detachment from the hostile world of ecclesiastical powers, see Winter, *Defecting in Place*. Similarly, Blow's call for boycotting the viewing or attending of the 2017 American presidential inauguration on the "impending

perhaps even because of [the kerygma's] apparent non-contextual character, Bultmann thereby elevates the call for a theology that is ever to be rethought, reformulated, and responsible in context."[46]

With the 2016 American presidential election bringing to the Oval Office a candidate whose crude rhetoric frequently belittled women, ethnic minorities, and immigrants under threat of deportation, while extolling national greatness, commending the use of state-sponsored torture, and praising authoritarian political leaders, we may find that to resist such atavistic appeals, not to mention the policies that may flow from them, contemporary Christians will need to recover something of what Bultmann meant in his time and place by a detaching *Entweltlichung*. Such "freedom from" the world may well be the first step in a new "freedom for" the world. As such, and in the paradoxical Paschal order of a "simultaneous sequence" of cross-resurrection, the conversion of homiletics to promissory kerygmatics may assist preachers and hearers of the Word to rethink and reformulate yet unknown material responses "under the compulsion of a concrete situation," one that we admittedly cannot fully anticipate or control, but one which faith can ever enter when accompanied by the promise and, hence, presence of Jesus Christ.

Day of Darkness" to "deprive it of oxygen and eyeballs; to plant a flag of resistance at the opening gate" captures something of the Pauline paradox of an intentional indifference that can matter in the public realm. See Blow, "The Anti-Inauguration," *The New York Times*, January 5, 2017.

46. Standhartinger, "Bultmann's Theology of the New Testament in Context," 255.

—6—

Promise as an Event of the Gospel in Context

Toward an Unfinished Homiletical Theology of Grace and Justice

—*David Schnasa Jacobsen*

> "[T]he most serious issue and task of a rhetoric of preaching is the allowing of the divine mystery to set language atremble."
>
> Edward Farley, *Practicing Gospel*

Homiletical theology is of at least two minds on promise. Promise is both a word of gracious presence and a word of coming justice.[1] To all those desiring to distinguish law and gospel, this wealth of promising approaches is rather confounding. At the same time, two quotes from Martin Luther

---

1. The premise for this presenting problem is based on various understandings of promise in homiletical theology in the work of colleagues James Kay, Eunjoo Mary Kim, David Lose, Dawn Ottoni Wilhelm, Kenyatta Gilbert, Paul Scott Wilson, Sally Brown, Christine Smith, and David Schnasa Jacobsen—as predicated in this consultation's guiding research question. In addition to these, other conceptions of a homiletical theology of promise are present as well in the work of Olin Moyd, Richard Lischer, Dale Andrews, and Ronald Allen and Joey Jeter, many of which I reference and describe more fully in "The Promise of Promise: Retrospect and Prospect of a Homiletical Theology," 3–16.

give me comfort when I reflect on this strange paradox of promise in the literature of my field. First, Luther promised his doctor's hat to anyone who could properly distinguish between law and gospel.[2] Such distinctions may be important, but also keep bumping up against the divine mystery, which makes any discernment far from easy in the theological task that is preaching. Second, Luther also had a unique take on what makes a theologian, precisely the (for our purposes in this volume, homiletical) one who must do all this distinguishing and discerning. What makes a theologian, Luther says, is "*Oratio, Meditatio, Tentatio*" or, prayer, meditation, and *suffering*."[3]

Luther's use of the word "suffering" does not necessarily have to raise any contemporary reader's hackles. I am not here invoking Luther's statement to prescribe suffering for anyone, least of all someone who benefits from less power and privilege than I do as a relatively comfortable United Methodist academic who lives in a nice Lutheran parsonage in the wooded suburbs of Boston. I am willing and in fact need to enter this process of talking about promise as a homiletical theology of the gospel in context with a degree of self-reflexivity about my privilege. However, I do want to take Luther's notion that suffering is related to good theology for descriptive rather than prescriptive reasons. This suffering, or *Tentatio* (*Anfechtung*), in Luther's saying is not some prescribed work, but a described reality of faith praxis. *Tentatio* or suffering here is not just about the anxious individual hoping for a gracious God, but a harried church struggling with gospel in context. This description of suffering places the Lutheran conception of promise, to my mind, in the context of personal and ecclesial praxis, in situations of suffering where promise is not just received (though it is), but also undergone, shared, and questioned in solidarity.

In this chapter I wish to think about the homiletical-theological task in relation to Oswald Bayer's unique understanding of promise as a speech act, which he views particularly in relation to lament and Luther's notion of the hiddenness of God.[4] Bayer links his notion of promise and lament deeply to *Anfechtung* or *Tentatio* as something believers "undergo" and a place where

---

2. This particular saying may well be apocryphal, even though fairly widely noted. Similar descriptions of the *difficult necessity* of discerning law and gospel show up in other parts of Luther's writings, especially his Table Talks and his sermons. Luther argues in Table Talk #1234 that only God in the Holy Spirit truly knows how to distinguish law and gospel, it is no human capacity and one that he himself is far from understanding in *Luther's Works* (Hereafter, *LW*) vol. 54, 127, similarly in his sermon on Gal 3:23–29 in *LW*, vol. 57, 67.

3. *LW* vol. 34, 285.

4. Bayer, *Martin Luther's Theology*. Joshua Miller does an excellent job of fleshing out these relationships in his *Hanging by a Promise*.

theologians are made.⁵ I wish to review and invert Bayer on this point of "undergoing." Along the way I will bring to the surface three important realities about promise that disrupt the ways in which one might normally discern a homiletical theology of the gospel in context. First, I understand promise with Bayer as in deep relation to lament, which has great impact on preaching practice. Promise animates a living faith in relation to both grace and justice, even as it invites believers into a theological tension. After all, grace is baffling because it is not always just. Moreover, justice is always problematizing what Bonhoeffer called cheap grace. I suggest that this very tension in the language of promise in preaching is unfinished theological business in the midst of *Anfechtung*. Second, I embrace promise not so much as an internal word, but as an external word.⁶ This external orientation, to my mind, pushes back on the typically epistemic turn in most deconstructive postmodern views of preaching that locate truth in the individual who testifies or confesses to promise or gospel. For me, promise is important not so much for epistemological reasons, but for reasons of *communion* as expressed in collaboration in the praxis of the *vita activa* (Arendt) and thus solidarity in *Anfechtung*—and this is precisely in contrast to Bayer's "undergoing" in what he calls the *vita passiva*.⁷ Promise for me exists to sustain human beings in relationship to God and with each other, not to put an epistemological Band-Aid on the Western problem of authority and knowledge. Third, promise is ultimately "undergone" in praxis, which is the point where the homiletical-theological task proper begins. For me, the central task and starting point of theological work, whether for preachers or homiletical scholars, is a "homiletical theology of the gospel in context." This "undergoing" of promise is for me precisely the "event" in which promise is named in the midst of struggle, as both the correlative of faith *and* hope. In calling this "undergoing" an event I am also taking up some of the unfinished theological business of the so-called new homiletic and placing this homiletical theology of promise in dialogue with recent philosophical reflections on

---

5. Bayer, *Martin Luther's Theology*, 19. In this context Bayer also distinguishes between academic theology and the worldly orientation of the theology of believers, but sees the two as being related precisely through the theologian's concern with *Oratio*, *Meditatio*, and *Tentatio*. The theologian does so to "give insight" to others in the same struggle.

6. Ibid., 252–53.

7. I add the work of Hannah Arendt here because of her concern with promise and the *vita activa*, especially with respect to her concern for action or praxis "among other humans" and in distinction from labor and work, *The Human Condition*, 7–21. In this way, I have made a departure from Bayer who understands the "undergoing" as part of the *vita passiva*. Even then, Arendt does talk about the intimate relationship of action and suffering (p. 190) in a way that almost resonates with Bayer's concern for *Anfechtung*, suffering, and "undergoing" the *vita passiva*.

event as it relates to the work of Slavoj Žižek, liturgical theologian Dirk Lange, and radical theologian John Caputo.

WHAT I MEAN BY HOMILETICAL THEOLOGY IN RELATION TO PROMISE

Gospel, Context and Theological Method

At the core of the task of homiletical theology is a coming to terms with some operative sense of the "gospel in context." André Resner's term, "working gospel," is a useful one insofar as it envisions both a strong sense of the gospel's character and a fundamentally dialogical way of relating to context.[8] Theologian Edward Farley set the terms for such a discussion in the field of homiletics when he argued that gospel is:

> . . . not a thing to be defined. It is not a doctrine, a delimited objective content. The summaries in Acts and in Paul of what is proclaimed, the formulas of the kerygma, attest to this. Phrases like the kingdom of God, Jesus as Lord, Christ crucified do have content, but that content is not simply a quantity of information. To proclaim means to bring to bear a certain past event on the present in such a way as to open the future. Since the present is always specific and situational, the way that the past, the event of Christ, is brought to bear so as to elicit hope will never be captured in some timeless phrase, some ideality of language. Preaching the good tidings is a new task whenever and wherever it takes place.[9]

In light of Farley's critique of the bridge paradigm, it becomes necessary to re-envision the field of homiletics as more than dealing with the *techne* of proper bridge building, but as a thoroughgoing theological enterprise. To my mind, it ends up placing both preacher and homiletician in the position of being theologians of the Word and not simply engineers who move from text to bridge to sermon.

Seminarians, practicing preachers and homileticians as scholars do not do this theological work in altogether the same way. This is why, I suspect, Charles Bartow carefully distinguishes between three kinds of homiletical theology (criticism): pedagogical, professional, and scholarly.[10] Pedagogical

---

8. Resner, "Preacher as God's Mystery Steward," 61–66.

9. Farley, *Practicing Gospel*, 80.

10. Charles Bartow, "Homiletical (Theological) Criticism," 154–57. What follows is my brief summary of Bartow's discussion.

refers to the more formative work which begins in the classroom. Here preachers become more intimately aware of preaching as a theological task, that the goal is somehow not reducible to just "preaching the text," but preaching gospel. It is perhaps also formative because this concern is related intimately to the *habitus* of doing theology itself, the disposition to reflect on the mysteries of God that serves as the kind of core of every believer's life, a kind of practical wisdom. Professional, says Bartow, refers to a more advanced way of thinking about such things that is the province of practicing preachers. Here, the practical wisdom or *habitus* becomes over time a part of the enlarged capacity of the preacher as theologian, through which a preacher becomes a truly reflective practitioner.[11] Scholarly homiletical theology is then essentially critical research at the service of the practice. Here homiletical theologians have the opportunity to dig more deeply into questions in relation to the traditions, contexts, cultures, and practices that shape preaching and are crucial for its working theological method. That is how I view the question here: how can a homiletical theology of promise serve as a core sense of the "gospel in context" today?

I have argued elsewhere that a theology of the gospel in context represents homiletical theology's core task. If, however, one wishes to see preaching as a thoroughgoing theological activity one cannot stop there. This is why I have argued that homiletical theology operates in several important "intersections" related to preaching's practices, cultures, and contexts. These also include theologies of preaching, theologies of Word and Sacrament, preaching as theological method generally, and theology in preaching.[12] My desire to identify these venues for doing homiletical theology is not exhaustive, just suggestive. If we homileticians take Wilson's "turn to theology" as an important moment for our field, it may just mean re-envisioning our work in a way that encompasses the breadth of scholarly homiletical theologians' concern.[13] Here I am not identifying something utterly new, but trying to push back on a solely methodological and technical view of preaching that too often occludes both its theological task and the many ways in which those theological concerns are already being pursued.

---

11. The language of *habitus* again echoes Farley's concern for understanding theology not solely as an academic genre, usually viewed as the province of the systematician, but as something that impacts all believers generally and contributes to theological understanding, along with theology as *scientia* or discipline, which becomes a forerunner to our conceptions of the term, *Theologia*, 32. Resner sometimes uses Gadamer's parallel language with the term "prejudice" to link this interpretive predisposition to his "working gospel," in "Do You See This Woman?" in *Theologies of the Gospel in Context*, 15–41.

12. Jacobsen, "Introduction," 10ff.

13. Wilson, "Is Homiletics Making a Theological Turn?," 15.

In this volume, however, our shared focus is on a working theology of the gospel as promise. Our working assumption in this chapter is that the gospel is not simply a delimited *theologoumenon*, but a mystery; or as Farley would put it, not a piece of information, but disclosing a "world of gospel." We might begin therefore by exploring how the gospel's character as promise is elaborated in the theology of Oswald Bayer and then consider what promise sounds like when it "undergoes" dialogue with context as part of its unfolding mystery, which preachers as theologians are called both to "serve" and to "steward" (1 Cor 4:1) with fidelity to the divine wisdom disclosed through Christ.

Promise and Lament by way of Luther's Hidden God

The move to consider promise *together with* lament would seem to be counterintuitive here. Yet what underlies the important relationship of promise and lament for Bayer is precisely his sense of divine mystery. Two key elements are the relationships of the hidden God to the revealed God and "God preached" to "God not preached." These relationships become the ground through which the promise is both articulated and undergone.

Bayer points out that Luther is careful to hold God's mystery close to hand. God has been revealed in the cross and resurrection of Jesus Christ, to be sure. Yet God is not fully revealed; God is still hidden.[14] Here Luther pushes back against some of the speculative moves of late medieval theology. God's omnipotence and God's strange work are to be neither mastered by human beings nor relativized. God is God; and we human beings are not. God remains both hidden and revealed—known, yes, through the crucifixion and resurrection, but still mysterious and hidden in the ways God's power is exercised and God's purposes brought to fruition.

This leads to another point of distinction for Luther that is important for his theology. There is both God preached and God not preached. God preached is the God disclosed in Jesus Christ, the One who is gracious toward us, the One through whom promise is both given and named. Human beings through the gospel lay hold of this God preached, even in the midst of difficulty, struggle, *Anfechtung*. Why? Because there is also God not preached, the great mystery who is beyond human knowing and understanding. The strange task of human beings in the presence of God is to lay hold of that gospel even in the face of the contradiction of God not preached. Joshua Miller puts it this way: "It is to this God alone that the sinner must flee when confronted

---

14. Bayer, *Martin Luther's Theology*, 11.

by the wrath of God experienced through a natural knowledge of God. The sinner must believe firmly, praying to God to save, hold 'God against God' to the promise of God's mercy in Christ against the wrath of the hidden God."[15]

Here it is important to make one thing especially clear: I am not joining in a claim for the startling, even terrifying, monism of a God responsible for both evil and good. Luther has his own reasons for pursuing his theology thusly. For me it suffices to embrace God's mystery along with a strong dose of human skepticism about what human beings in the presence of God do know. There is for me a flipside to mystery that is important for a homiletical theology to maintain. Mysteries may well be something still to be fully revealed—they point to a more final eschatological unveiling. Still, for now, homiletical theologians remain bound by the eschatological *proviso*: "For now we see through a glass, darkly; but then face to face" (1 Cor 13:12, KJV).

FROM LUTHER TO BAYER

Promise and Lament in Relation to God Preached and God Not Preached

This ground in God hidden and revealed, God preached and not preached, is important for Bayer's understanding of promise. Bayer builds his notion on Austin's theory of speech acts in *How to Do Things with Words*.[16] The importance, for Bayer, is that a promise is not a premise. A premise or proposition is a statement behind which something stands, and to which it refers. Such statements Austin refers to as "constatives." By contrast, promise is an example of a different kind of speech, one focused not on some reality behind the word, but a reality which is created by a word. A promise is thus, according to Austin, a *performative* utterance.[17] Rather than point to some reality or state behind itself, a promise is the thing itself—the reality is the sign—or better, creates a relationship. Bayer writes, "'I promise you' . . . does not refer to a preexisting situation whose existence the sentence merely reveals. Rather, it constitutes and creates a relationship and incorporates features that are both personal

---

15. Joshua Miller, *Hanging by a Promise*, 22. The quoted wording from Luther comes in part from *LW* 19:17, 72.

16. Austin, *How to Do Things with Words*. Other scholars have noted the difficulty of appropriating Austin's work as well as speech act theory for making broad theological claims—in part because Austin's theory is not always consistent, see Briggs, *Speech Act Theory and Biblical Interpretation*, 6–10 and 38ff.

17. Austin, *How to Do Things*, 9–11.

and objective."[18] Although Bayer does not mention this in his own writing, the work of Donald Evans carries a similar notion even further by focusing on the "self-involvement of the promiser" in the speech act itself.[19] In this sense, potentially a deeply Lutheran sense, promise and faith are intimately related and connected to a kind of *presence* of the promiser.

Yet what makes Bayer's contribution so significant is his relation of promise and faith to the very *Anfechtung* of believers in relation to God hidden and revealed. Joshua Miller describes it in a way that is crucial for the kind of "unfinished" homiletical theology I am envisioning:

> ... Bayer argues that the experience that makes a theologian is not only the experience of God through the promise in Christ but also the general experience of God outside of the gracious revelation of God in Christ. This general experience of God, which occurs through creation itself, presents God to the human in terrifying hiddenness (*schreckliche Verborgenheit*). This hiddenness grips the believer through *Anfechtung*, helping to make him or her into a theologian. At least in part, it is the experience of God through the terrifying hiddenness evident in the evil things that happen in the world, through human and non-human means, which constitutes the experience that makes one a theologian.[20]

What is curious about this, however, is not just the strange mystery it attaches to promise and divine revelation, but the unique problem it poses for doing theology and distinguishing law and gospel. For Bayer, says Miller, God's hiddenness represents a "third form of God's address" to humans beyond law and gospel.[21] This to my mind has profound implications for how one thinks about homiletical theology's "unfinished task."

Bayer's approach also reconfigures the way in which promise relates to the provisional nature of the human language of proclamation. While the relationship of the divine and human elements of promise has been treated in the work of the philosopher Nicholas Wolterstorff, who sees it as a form of "double agency" in speech made possible by splitting the locutionary and illocutionary elements between human and divine agents,[22] less has been said about the human element of promise in light of the postmodern shift to the provisionality of human language generally. This provisionality hinges in part

---

18. Bayer, *Theology the Lutheran Way*, 128.
19. Evans, *The Logic of Self-involvement*.
20. Miller, *Hanging by a Promise*, 206.
21. Ibid., 207.
22. Wolterstorff, *Divine* Discourse.

on the radical suspicion of human language and its capacity for reference outside of human speech claims. This, in turn, has a huge impact on conceptions of faith in that the truth of the statement is then relegated to an internal referent. Philosopher Phillip Cary has highlighted a similar issue with respect to Calvinist and Lutheran conceptions of the syllogism of justification:[23] Justification is by grace through faith, I know that I am justified because I know that I believe, therefore I am justified—or—Justification is by grace through faith, I know that I am justified because God is not a liar, therefore I am justified. What Carey points out with these two syllogisms is a classic distinction between Calvin and Luther's warrants for justifying faith. What underlies the distinction is the unique commitments concerning the internal and external word with the Reformers. With Luther, the external word is key and God is its guarantor. The "mis-fire" or "infelicity" of the promise is not "I do not believe," but "God must be a liar."[24]

This relative reliance on the external word becomes, then, key for Bayer's own interest in setting promise in relationship to lament. Just as promise is something to which one holds in the face of *Anfechtung* or even the mysterious hidden God, lament is a way of holding promise back to God in theological engagement. What Bayer calls the "bodily" word may not be confused with the divine Word which does its work as promise,[25] as divine speech act—it is grace all the way down! Still, the external or bodily word is the means by which the divine promise is made and made effectual: in Word and Sacrament.[26] It is the word in this externalized sense that grounds the promise *and* allows believers to lay hold of the promise in the midst of injustice, suffering, and *Anfechtung*. Lament is a faithful act of believers who act *based* on the gift of the promise itself, its given-ness as external word. Lament acknowledges the contradiction of the promise in this apocalyptically ruptured age, yet it also lays hold of the promise in trusting the revealed God on the way to eschatological fulfillment of the promise, in the very face of suffering and the hidden God.

---

23. I treat this issue more fully in my article, "The Promise of Promise," 5–6. My summary here is a further reflection based on Cary's work on the promise viewed externally and internally in Phillip Cary, "*Sola Fide:* Luther and Calvin," 266.

24. The notion is corroborated in Bayer's own work in *Theology the Lutheran Way*, 129–31, where he writes of the efficacy of the (performative) external word, the spoken promise of Biblical texts and sacramental actions.

25. Miller, *Hanging by a Promise*, 157.

26. Bayer, *Theology the Lutheran Way*, 90.

PECCATA FORTE: BEYOND BAYER'S VITA PASSIVA TO ARENDT'S VITA ACTIVA

At this point, however, I openly part ways with the Lutheran Bayer. My own contradiction as an admitted "Luthodist" is to hold together a high view of justification by grace through faith and a vestigial sense of Wesleyan social holiness. I wish to expand Bayer's vision right here to press beyond the *vita passiva* by which promise works both faith and hope to argue, based on a praxis-oriented revision of Bayer that seeks to read the life of faith in promise as its own unique *vita activa* from the work of the philosopher Hannah Arendt. In doing so, I believe I do carry forward Luther's understanding of *Anfechtung* as related to ecclesial praxis around the gospel, although I am unwilling to concede that the faith and hope that promise arouses, when related to the sphere of human action, is just one more "work." For me, promise is itself the activating force, the empowering lever by which grace pries open a seemingly closed creation to its promised newness in the gospel in context. Such good news does not ultimately fix the world, but it does pry it open with God's proleptic newness so as to make a way forward where there was none before. It is in this sense both theo-centric *and* enmeshed in praxis, the very sphere of *Anfechtung* as it relates to gospel—a clearing of communion, collaboration, and solidarity made available as a living extension of the "bodily word" of the revealed God amidst the terrifying hiddenness of gospel persecution, injustice, and suffering.

My perspective clearly goes beyond Bayer who draws a sharp distinction between present and future, presence and fullness. His view of lament embraces a radical divine solidarity of creation and Holy Spirit, but yields a human waiting for divine action.[27] Yet I am convinced that the performative nature of promise does more than promote faith in the *vita passiva* sense that Bayer embraces. Promise, as I have claimed elsewhere, offers both presence and *discloses* a future in such a way as to pry creation just a bit more open. Walter Brueggemann puts an analogous view of promise in *Cadences of Home*:

> . . .promises, specific as they are, are cast as God's own speech, the authority for which is not found in any visible circumstance but in the trustworthiness of the God who speaks. It is God's own resolve to work a newness that will impinge upon what seems to be a closed, hopeless situation.

---

27. Bayer, *Theology the Lutheran Way*, 212–13. For a fuller treatment of the various theological dimensions of this and their relation to lament, see Miller, *Hanging by a Promise*, 244–54.

Toward a Homiletical Theology of Promise

> ... Promise has become nearly an alien category among us. That is partly an intellectual problem for us, because our Enlightenment perception of reality does not believe that there can be any newness "from the outside" that can enter our fixed world. The loss of promise is also a function of our privilege in the world, whereby we do not in fact want newness, but only an enhancement and guarantee of our preferred present tense.[28]

Promise, in other words, is the incalculable from the outside. "I will do X," says God and already begins acting on the present. Both the promiser and the promise are becoming present in the moment. To my mind, the illocutionary function of promise is thus not related solely to the self-involvement of the promiser, which manifests even now a Presence. It may offer a possiblilizing *arrabon*, a down payment on justice, a "first fruits" of the promise in the Spirit whose reality intrudes even now in connection with the promiser. Philosopher Richard Kearney tries to describe this in what he calls possibilizing "onto-eschatological" terms: God is a traversing presence, like the voice from the burning bush at Sinai, who is who [God] will be.[29] Such a view breaks open the fixed realities of ontology which the new homiletic tried at points to extract from the late Heidegger and the new hermeneutic of Fuchs and Ebeling.[30] Kearney's possibilizing view of promise also pushes back against the endless *deferral* of both the promiser and the promise in the Derridean "radical theology" of John Caputo or a purely deconstructive homiletic that places both divine grace and justice in a kind of hall of mirrors constructed out of parentheses, brackets, and ellipses.[31]

Such an onto-eschatological view of promise may just be enough as a "bodily word," an external word, capable of bearing the promise of the Promiser. This possibilizing view requires a strange juxtaposition of the "is" and the "ought," the "now" and the "will be." Like communion, it bears witness to promise as both forgiveness and hope amidst stained glass and even mainline, middle-class dislodged privilege and traumatic brokenness, too. Its embodied-ness does not point to human achievement, but divine action in the midst of Eucharistic practice, a promising sign that both announces grace

---

28. Brueggemann, *Cadences of Home*, 22–23.

29. Kearney, *The God Who May Be*, chapter 1.

30. While some representatives of the new homiletic build a view of gospel as event of experience, drawing on a kind of Heideggerian ontology connected with Tillich's theology, it is interesting that Fuchs and Ebeling themselves have not abandoned by any means the more specific language of promise: Ebeling, *The Nature of Faith*, 190 and *Word and Faith*, 327 as well as Fuchs, *Studies of the Historical Jesus*, 94–95.

31. Caputo, *The Insistence of God*, 2013.

and pries open provisional justice in ecclesial praxis. Precisely at those points where ecclesial communities are bound up in oppressive relations and broken identities, the promise intrudes and traverses the sphere of human action and *Anfechtung*.

From the human side of promise, philosopher Hannah Arendt offers some sense of what this might look like in praxis. Maurizio Passerin d'Entrèves describes Arendt's work this way:

> The remedy which the tradition of Western thought has proposed for the unpredictability and irreversibility of action has consisted in abstaining from action altogether, in the withdrawal from the sphere of interaction with others, in the hope that one's freedom and integrity could thereby be preserved. Platonism, Stoicism and Christianity elevated the sphere of contemplation above the sphere of action, precisely because in the former one could be free from the entanglements and frustrations of action. Arendt's proposal, by contrast, is not to turn one's back on the realm of human affairs, but to rely on two faculties inherent in action itself, the faculty of forgiving and the faculty of promising. These two faculties are closely connected, the former mitigating the irreversibility of action by absolving the actor from the unintended consequences of his or her deeds, the latter moderating the uncertainty of its outcome by binding actors to certain courses of action and thereby setting some limit to the unpredictability of the future. Both faculties are, in this respect, connected to *temporality*: from the standpoint of the present forgiving looks backward to what has happened and absolves the actor from what was unintentionally done, while promising looks forward as it seeks to establish islands of security in an otherwise uncertain and unpredictable future.[32]

Here, with Wolterstorff's double-agency of promise speech, it embodies at the level of praxis what James Kay has called the correlative of faith[33]—and perhaps even hope. The process, however, calls for theologians who receive promise in the midst of *Anfechtung*, divine action within the very "wound" of ecclesial praxis.

What I envision methodologically is something analogous to the praxis-based approach to gospel reflection and action developed in *Kairos Preaching*:

---

32. Passerin d'Entreves, "Hannah Arendt," Entry 4.5.

33. Kay, *Preaching and Theology*, 121 is where Kay makes the most explicit statement of the promise/faith correlative. Teasingly on p. 61, in an interesting reading of Martin Luther King's Christmas sermon, Kay opens up the possibility of an analogous relationship to hope.

Toward a Homiletical Theology of Promise

Speaking Gospel to the Situation.[34] Promise provokes both reflection and action, while reflection and action return preachers (and hearers) to promise as theologians—it is in this sense, as Resner calls it, "working gospel." In the moment, such contextual dialogue becomes the space where the character of gospel as promise bumps up against realities which alternately sponsor profound trust, sometimes fist-shaking lament, and in bits and pieces faithful/hopeful praxis even now. Here the *event* of the gospel is not its ontological disclosure through language, but the promise's "undergoing" in the midst of *Anfechtung*, that is in the context of *praxis*. Why event? Slavoj Žižek argues that the power of such a speech act is that it becomes a "symbolic event" in the way that it opens up such a new reality and "restructures an entire field."[35] John Caputo speaks of promise as an "event" that is both Deleuzean and Derridean in character: as something unforeseen that is both "virtual" and "disruptive." Most tellingly liturgical theologian Dirk Lange sees promise as an event of return, a kind of working through of promise tied to the its dissemination in a Eucharistic act that reorients believers "in relation to event, context, and self." In my view the event of promise in context is a kind of "undergoing" in which promise is heard in relation to *Anfechtung*, life lived in the context of praxis. Such a moment sets loose a moment of theological naming and reflection in relation to promise which is ever unfinished. It is unfinished in being new in every moment—a reality which Farley has named prominently in the extended quote above. Yet it is also unfinished in another sense: in that the promise is something theologians and believers both continually hear and undergo in the midst of struggle. When preachers leave room for that dialogue in preaching, *gospel* is more than a content, more even than a disclosure of being through language; it is also an event in context, in *praxis*, even in *Anfechtung*.

It is in the struggle with promise that homiletical theology emerges out of its unfinished task, like Jacob at the Jabbok, with both a blessing and a limp. Such is not enough to fix all the problems with Esau, but is sufficient to still go and meet him as called forward by the promise—even as he is hindered by his own scheming and brokenness. Promise is a speech act that bears witness to a theo-centric reality begetting both faith and hope, yet it is bodily in that its double agency creates spaces as a bodied word that carries forward both the Promiser and the promise. In this way it quite possibly bends reality even

---

34. Both co-author Kelly and I developed a praxis-oriented hermeneutical circle that begins with gospel and moves toward change at the level of action, in *Kairos Preaching*, 14–20. The priority of promise is given with the very praxis-oriented dialogical model whose starting point is "gospel" in a context. Both of us place ourselves in the praxis model of contextual theology outlined by Bevans in his book *Models of Contextual Theology*, 2002.

35. Žižek, *Event*, 124.

now in small ways toward God's ultimate purposes—as Arendt might describe them here beyond her own anthropological vision, "islands of certainty in an ocean of uncertainty."[36]

In such moments, a homiletical theology of promise in context will exist precisely in tension between the two forms it takes in preaching: as grace and justice. Yet in its pedagogical form as students boldly name promise and hesitate at its implications, that disruptive tension can provide a deeper texture to preaching gospel even as the struggle ensues. This homiletical theology of promise in context will be familiar to reflective practitioners who do their work in a professional mode as the word of promise both comes and stands in tension with the lived experiences pastors know all too well require an undergoing of promise in praxis. From there, it can be a bold means of naming promise ever anew in the world. Among those of us in this volume who pursue homiletical theology in a scholarly mode, it breaks loose in a more sober, critically-reflective wisdom that holds on to promise even while it struggles with its naming as a mystery that sets our words "atremble."

---

36. Arendt, *Human Condition*, 244.

Bibliography

Allen, Ron J. ed., *Patterns of Preaching: A Sermon Sampler*. St. Louis: Chalice, 1998.
Allmen, Jean-Jacques von. *Preaching and Congregation*. London: SCM, 1962.
Althaus-Reid, Maria Marcella, and Lisa Isherwood. *Controversies in Feminist Theology*. London: SCM, 2007.
Andrews, Dale A. *Practical Theology for Black Churches: Bridging Black Theology and African American Folk Religion*. Louisville: Westminster John Knox, 2002.
Arendt, Hannah. *The Human Condition*. Chicago: The University of Chicago Press, 1998.
Attridge, Harold W. *The Epistle to the Hebrews: a Commentary on the Epistle to the Hebrews*. Hermeneia: a Critical and Historical Commentary on the Bible. Philadelphia: Fortress, 1989.
Augustine. *City of God*. Translated by Henry Bettenson. London: Penguin, 1972.
———. *Confessions*. Translated by Henry Chadwick. New York: Oxford University Press, 1991.
———. *On Christian Doctrine*. Translated by D. W. Robertson. Upper Saddle River, NJ: Prentice Hall, 1958
Austin, J. L. *How to Do Things with Words*. Cambridge, MA: Harvard University Press, 1962.
———. "Performative Utterances [1956]." In *Philosophical Papers*, 220–39. Oxford: Clarendon, 1961.
Baker, Christopher. *The Hybrid Church in the City*. Aldershot, UK: Ashgate, 2007.
Barth, Karl. *Homiletik: Wesen und Vorbereitung der Predigt*. Zürich: Theologischer Verlag, 1970.
———. "The Need and Promise of Christian Preaching." In *The Word of God and the Word of Man*, 97–135. New York: Harper and Row, 1928.
Bartholomew, Craig G. *Where Mortals Dwell: A Christian View of Place for Today*. Grand Rapids: Baker Academic, 2011.
Bartow, Charles. "Homiletical (Theological) Criticism." In *The New Interpreter's Handbook of Preaching*, edited by P. Wilson, 154–57. Nashville: Abingdon, 2008.
Bayer, Oswald. *Martin Luther's Theology: A Contemporary Interpretation*. Translated by Thomas H. Trapp. Grand Rapids: Eerdmans, 2008.
———. *Theology the Lutheran Way*. Translated and edited by Jeffrey G. Silcock and Mark C. Mattes. Grand Rapids: Eerdmans, 2007.
Becker, Carl L. *The Heavenly City of the Eighteenth-Century Philosophers*. New Haven: Yale University Press, 1932.
Bevans, Stephen B. *Models of Contextual Theology*. Maryknoll, NY: Orbis, 2002.

Bibliography

Bhabha, Homi K. "Cultures in Between." In *Questions of Cultural Identity*, edited by Stuart Hall and Paul du Gay, 53–60. London, Sage, 1996.

———. "Frontlines/Borderposts." In *Displacements: Cultural Identities in Question*, edited by Angelica Bammer, 269–73. Bloomington, Indiana University Press, 1994.

———. *The Location of Culture*. London: Routledge, 1994.

Blair, Hugh. *Lectures on Rhetoric and Belles Lettres*. 1783. Reprint, Delmar: Scholars' Facimiles and Pamphlets, 1993.

Boer, Roland, and Fernando F. Segovia. "Introduction: The Futures of Biblical Pasts." In *The Future of the Biblical Past: Envisioning Global Studies on a Global Key*, edited by Roland Boer and Fernando F. Segovia. *Society of Biblical Literature*, Semeia Series, No. 66 (2012). www.sbl-site.org/assets/pdfs/pubs/060666P.front.pdf.

Boulton, Matthew Myer. "The Adversary: Agony, Irony, and the Liturgical Role of the Holy Spirit," In *The Spirit in Worship-Worship in the Spirit*, edited by Teresa Berger and Bryan D. Spinks, 59–78. Collegeville, MN: Liturgical Press, 2009.

Brettler, Marc Zvi. "The Future of Biblical Studies," *SBL Forum*. http://sbl-site.org/Article.aspx?ArticleID=320.

Briggs, Richard S. *Words in Action: Speech Act Theory and Biblical Interpretation*. Edinburgh: T & T Clark, 2001.

Brueggemann, Walter. *A Commentary on Jeremiah: Exile and Homecoming*. Grand Rapids: Eerdmans, 1998.

———. *Cadences of Home: Preaching among Exiles*. Louisville: Westminster John Knox, 1997.

Buechner, Fredrick. *Telling the Truth: The Gospel as Tragedy, Comedy and Fairy Tale*. San Francisco: Harper and Row, 1977.

Bultmann, Rudolf. "*Allgemeine Wahrheiten und christliche Verkündingung* [1957]." In *Glauben und Verstehen*, 166–77. Tübingen: Mohr/ Siebeck, 1993.

———. "Introduction." In Adolf von Harnack, *What Is Christianity?* Translated by Thomas Bailey Saunders, vii–xviii. New York: Harper, 1957.

———. *Jesus Christ and Mythology*. New York: Scribner, 1958.

———. "On the Problem of Demythologizing." In *New Testament and Mythology and Other Basic Writings*, edited by Schubert M. Ogden, 95–130. Philadelphia: Fortress, 1989.

———. "Reply." In *The Theology of Bultmann*, edited by Charles W. Kegley, 257–87. New York: Harper & Row, 1966.

———. "The Primitive Christian Kerygma and the Historical Jesus" In *The Historical Jesus and the Kerygmatic Christ*, edited and translated by Carl E. Braaten and Roy A. Harrisville, 15–42. New York: Abingdon, 1964.

———. *Theologie des Neuen Testaments*, edited by Otto Merk. Tübingen: Mohr/Siebeck, 1984.

———. *Theology of the New Testament*. Translated by Kendrick Grobel, 3 vols. New York: Scribner, 1951–1955.

Burghardt, S.J., Walter J. *Preaching the Just Word*. New Haven: Yale University Press, 1996.

Bushnell, Horace. "Our Gospel, a Gift to the Imagination," In *Horace Bushnell: Sermons*, edited by Conrad Cherry, 95–117. New York: Paulist, 1985.

Buttrick, David. *Homiletic: Moves and Structures*. Minneapolis: Fortress, 1987.

———. *Preaching the New and the Now*. Louisville: Westminster John Knox, 1998.

Cannon, Katie Geneva. *Teaching Preaching: Isaac Rufus Clark and Black Sacred Rhetoric*. New York: Continuum, 2002.

Bibliography

Caputo, John. *The Insistence of God: A Theology of Perhaps.* Bloomington: Indiana University Press, 2013.
Carter, J. Kameron. *Race: A Theological Account.* New York: Oxford University Press, 2008.
Cary, Phillip. "Sola Fide: Luther and Calvin," *Concordia Theological Quarterly* 71 (July/October 2007) 265–281.
Caspari, W. "Homiletik." In *Für protestantische Theologie und Kirche*, Vol. 8. 3rd ed., 295–308. Leipzig: Hinrich, 1900.
Chauvet, Louis-Marie. *Symbol and Sacrament: A Sacramental Reinterpretation of Christian Existence.* Translated by Patrick Madigan and Madeleine Beaumont. Collegeville, MN: Liturgical Press, 1990.
Choy, Wilbur W. Y. "Strangers Called to Mission." In *Churches Aflame: Asian Americans and United Methodism*, edited by Artemio R. Guillermo, 65–89. Nashville: Abingdon, 1991.
Clark, Mary T. *Augustine of Hippo, Selected Writings.* New York: Paulist Press, 1984.
Cmiel, Kenneth. *Democratic Eloquence: The Fight over Popular Speech in Nineteenth-Century America.* Los Angeles: University of California Press, 1990.
Coakley, Sarah. *God, Sexuality, and the Self: An Essay 'On the Trinity.'* Cambridge, UK: Cambridge University Press, 2013.
Cone, James H. *Black Theology and Black Power.* New York: Orbis, 1969.
Congdon, David W. *The God Who Saves: A Dogmatic Sketch.* Eugene, OR: Cascade, 2016.
———. *The Mission of Demythologizing: Rudolf Bultmann's Dialectical Theology.* Minneapolis: Fortress, 2015.
———. *Rudolf Bultmann: A Companion to His Theology.* Eugene, OR: Cascade, 2015.
Craddock, Fred B. *As One Without Authority.* Nashville: Abingdon, 1979.
———. *Craddock on the Craft of Preaching*, edited by Lee Sparks and Kathryn Hayes Sparks. St. Louis: Chalice, 2011.
Das, Man Singh. "Sojourners in the Land of the Free: History of Southern Asian United Methodist Churches." In *Churches Aflame: Asian Americans and United Methodism*, edited by Artemio R. Guillermo, 19–34. Nashville: Abingdon, 1991.
Davis, Henry Grady. *Design for Preaching.* Philadelphia: Fortress, 1958.
Dix, Gregory. *The Shape of the Liturgy.* San Francisco: Harper & Row, 1982.
Dodd, C. H. *The Apostolic Preaching and Its Developments: Three Lectures, with an Appendix on Eschatology and History.* New York: Harper & Brothers, 1962.
Du Bois, W. E. B. et al. *The Souls of Black Folk Essays and Sketches.* Charlottesville, VA: University of Virginia Library, 1996.
Dumas, André. *Dietrich Bonhoeffer, Theologian of Reality.* New York: Macmillan, 1971.
Dyas, Dee. "Exile and Pilgrimage." In *A Dictionary of Biblical Tradition in English Literature*, edited by David L. Jeffrey, 254–59. Grand Rapids: Eerdmans, 1992.
———. *Pilgrimage in Medieval English Literature, 700–1500.* Rochester, NY: Brewer, 2001.
Ebeling, Gerhard. *The Nature of Faith.* Translated by Ronald G. Smith. Philadelphia: Fortress, 1961.
———. *Word and Faith.* Translated by James W. Leitch. Philadelphia: Fortress, 1963.
Evans, Donald D. *The Logic of Self-Involvement: A Philosophical Study of Everyday Language with Special Reference to the Christian Use of Language about God as Creator.* London: SCM, 1963.
Evans, James H. *We Have Been Believers: an African American Systematic Theology*, 2nd ed. Minneapolis: Fortress, 2012.
Farley, Edward. *Practicing Gospel.* Louisville: Westminster John Knox, 2004.

Bibliography

———. *Theologia: The Fragmentation and Unity of Theological Education*. Philadelphia: Fortress, 1982.

Fuchs, Ernst. *Studies of the Historical Jesus*. London: SCM, 1961.

Gilbert, Kenyatta R. *The Journey and Promise of African American Preaching*. Minneapolis: Augsburg, 2011.

———. *A Pursued Justice: Black Preaching from the Great Migration to Civil Rights*. Waco, TX: Baylor University Press, 2016.

Gilbert, Kenyatta R., and AnneMarie Mingo. "The Preached Word: Holistic Practices in the Urban/Suburban South (Metropolitan Atlanta, Georgia)." In *Equipping the Saints: Promising Practices in Black Churches and Communities—A Resource Guide*, edited by Alton B. Pollard III and Velma E. Love, 8–17. Howard University School of Divinity, ETS: Promising Practices in Black Congregational Life, National Research Project, The Lilly Endowment, Inc. (May 2015).

Graves, Mike. *The Sermon as Symphony: Preaching the Literary Forms of the New Testament*. Valley Forge, PA: Judson, 1997.

Greenhaw, David M., and Ronald Allen. *Preaching in the Context of Worship*. St. Louis: Chalice, 2000.

Hall, Douglas John. *Professing the Faith: Christian Theology in a North American Context*. Minneapolis: Fortress, 1993.

Hammann, Konrad. *Rudolf Bultmann: A Biography*. Translated by Phillip E. Devenish. Salem, OR: Polebridge, 2013.

Hauerwas, Stanley, and William H. Willimon. *Resident Aliens: Life in the Christian Colony*, 25th anniversary ed. Nashville: Abingdon, 2014.

Hogan, Lucy Lind, and Robert Reid. *Connecting with the Congregation: Rhetoric and the Art of Preaching*. Nashville: Abingdon, 1999.

Jacobsen, David Schnasa. "Introduction." In *Homiletical Theology: Preaching as Doing Theology*, 3–19. Eugene, OR: Cascade, 2015.

———. "The Promise of Promise: Retrospect and Prospect of a Homiletical Theology." *Homiletic* 38, no. 2 (2013) 3–16.

———. "What is Homiletical Theology? An Invitation to Constructive Theological Dialogue in North American Homiletics." In *Homiletical Theology: Preaching as Doing Theology*, edited by David S. Jacobsen, 23–38. Eugene, OR: Cascade, 2015.

Jacobsen, David Schnasa, and Robert Kelly. *Kairos Preaching: Speaking Gospel to the Situation*. Minneapolis: Fortress, 2009.

Jennings, Willie. "The Aesthetic Struggle and Ecclesial Vision." In *Black Practical Theology*, 163–85. Waco: Baylor, 2015.

Jensen, Robert. *The Heart of Whiteness: Confronting Race, Racism and White Privilege*. San Francisco: City Lights, 2005.

Jeter, Joseph R. "A Development of Poetic Preaching: a Slice of History," *Homiletic* 15 (Winter 1990) 5–12.

Josuttis, Manfred. *Rhetorik und Theologie in der Predigtarbeit: Homiletischen Studien*. München: Chr. Kaiser Verlag, 1985.

Kavanagh, Aidan. *On Liturgical Theology*. New York: Pueblo, 1984.

Kay, James F. *Christus Praesens: A Reconsideration of Rudolf Bultmann's Christology*. Grand Rapids: Eerdmans, 1994.

———. *Preaching and Theology*. St. Louis: Chalice, 2007.

Kearney, Richard. *The God Who May Be: A Hermeneutics of Religion*. Bloomington: Indiana University Press, 2001.

Bibliography

Keller, Catherine. *Apocalypse Now and Then: A Feminist Guide to the End of the World*. Boston: Beacon, 1996.

Kim, Eunjoo. *Preaching in an Age of Globalization*. Louisville: Westminster John Knox, 2010.

———. *Preaching the Presence of God: A Homiletic from an Asian American Perspective*. Valley Forge, PA: Judson, 1999.

Knight. Henry H. *Anticipating Heaven Below: Optimism of Grace from Wesley to the Pentecostals*. Eugene, OR: Cascade, 2014.

Knowles, Michael P. *Of Seeds and the People of God: Preaching as Parable, Crucifixion, and Testimony*. Eugene, Oregon: Cascade, 2015.

Koester, Craig. *Hebrews*. Anchor Yale Bible, Vol. 36. New York: Doubleday, 2001.

Kwok, Pui-lan. *Postcolonial Imagination and Feminist Theology*. Louisville: Westminster John Knox, 2005.

———. "Postcolonial Preaching in Intercultural Contexts." *Homiletic* 40 (2015) 8–21.

Lamb, Matthew. *Solidarity with Victims: Toward a Theology of Social Transformation*. New York: Crossroad, 1982.

Lathrop, Gordon. *Holy Things: A Liturgical Theology*. Minneapolis: Fortress, 1993.

Lee, Jung Young. *Korean Preaching: An Interpretation*. Nashville: Abingdon, 1997.

Lee, Sang Hyun. *From a Liminal Place: An Asian American Theology*. Minneapolis: Fortress, 2010.

———. "Pilgrimage and Home in the Wilderness of Marginality: Symbols and Context in Asian American Theology." In *Korean Americans and Their Religions: Pilgrims and Missionaries from a Different Shore*, edited by Ho-Youn Kwon et al., 55–69. University Park: Pennsylvania State University, 2001.

Leith, John H. *Basic Christian Doctrine*. Louisville: Westminster John Knox, 1993.

Levinas, Emmanuel. *Otherwise Than Being, or Beyond Essence*. Translated by Alphonso Lingis. Pittsburgh: Duquesne University Press, 1998.

Lew, Jiwhang. "The Korean Church as a Polis: A Theological Contextualization of St. Augustine's Political Thought." *The Asia Journal of Theology* 15 (October 2001) 324–47.

———. "Politics of Virtue: St. Augustine's political thought considered for the Korean Church in national division." PhD diss., Northwestern University, 2000.

Linklater, Kristin. *Freeing Shakespeare's Voice*. New York: Theatre Communications Group, 1992.

———. *Freeing the Natural Voice*, Revised and Expanded ed. Hollywood, CA: Drama, 2006.

Loder, James E. "Normativity and Context in Practical Theology: The Interdisciplinary Issue." In *Practical Theology: International Perspectives*, edited by Friedrich Schweitzer and Johannes A. Van der Ven Beren, 359–81. Frankfort am Main: Peter Lang, 1999.

Long, Thomas G. *Preaching and the Literary Forms of the Bible*. Philadelphia: Fortress, 1989.

———. *The Witness of Preaching*, 2nd ed. Louisville: Westminster John Knox, 2005.

Lopez, Davina C., and Penner, Todd. "Emerging Approaches in New Testament Studies." In *Oxford Bibliographies* 18 (June 2015). http://www.oxfordbibliographies.com/view/document/obo-9780195393361/obo-9780195393361-0081.xml.

Loscalzo, Craig A. *Preaching Sermons That Connect: Effective Communication Through Identification*. Downers Grove: InterVarsity, 1992.

Bibliography

Lund, Eric. *Documents from the History of Lutheranism, 1517–1750*. Minneapolis: Fortress, 2002.
Luther, Martin. *Luther's Works*, vol. 34, edited by L. Spitz. Philadelphia: Muhlenberg, 1960.
———. *Luther's Works*, vol. 54, edited by T. Tappert. Philadelphia: Fortress, 1967.
———. *Luther's Works*, vol. 57, edited by B. Mayes. St. Louis: Concordia, 2016.
Matsuoka, Fumitaka. *Out of Silence: Emerging Themes in Asian American Churches*. Eugene, OR: Wipf & Stock, 2009.
McConville Gordon, et al. *Explorations in Christian Theology of Pilgrimage*, edited by Craig G. Bartholomew and Fred Hughes. Burlington, VT: Ashgate, 2003.
McKenzie, Alyce M. "The Company of Sages: Homiletical Theology as a Sapiential Hermeneutic." In *Homiletical Theology: Preaching as Doing Theology, The Promise of Homiletical Theology, V.1*, edited by David Jacobsen. 87–102. Eugene, OR: Cascade, 2015.
———. *Preaching Biblical Wisdom in a Self-Help Society*. Nashville: Abingdon, 2002.
———. *Preaching Proverbs: Wisdom for the Pulpit*. Louisville: Westminster John Knox, 1996.
McMaken, W. Travis. "Definitive, Defective or Deft? Reassessing Barth's Doctrine of Baptism in *Church Dogmatics* IV/4." *International Journal of Systematic Theology* 17 (January 2015) 89–114.
Micks, Marianne H. *The Future Present: The Phenomenon of Christian Worship*. New York: Seabury, 1970.
Miller, Joshua. *Hanging by a Promise: The Hidden God in the Theology of Oswald Bayer*. Eugene, OR: Pickwick, 2015.
Mitchell, Henry H. *Celebration and Experience in Preaching*. Revised edition. Nashville: Abingdon, 2008.
Moltmann, Jürgen. *Experiences in Theology: Ways and Forms of Christian Theology*. Minneapolis: Fortress, 2000.
———. *Theology of Hope: On the Ground and the Implications of a Christian Eschatology*. London: SCM, 1967.
Mosheim, Johann Lorenz von. *Anweisung erbaulich zu predigen*, edited by C. E. von Winheim. Erlangen: Bey Wolfgang Walther. 1762.
Morrill, Bruce T. *Anamnesis as Dangerous Memory: Political and Liturgical Theology in Dialogue*. Collegeville, MN: Liturgical Press, 2000.
———., ed. *Bodies of Worship: Explorations in Theory and Practice*. Collegeville: Liturgical Press, 1999.
Morse, Christopher. *The Difference Heaven Makes: Rehearing the Gospel as News*. New York: T & T Clark, International, 2010.
———. *The Logic of Promise in Moltmann's Theology*. Philadelphia: Fortress, 1979.
Nagano, Paul M. "A Japanese American Pilgrimage: Theological Reflections." In *Journeys at the Margin: Toward an Autobiographical Theology in American-Asian Perspective*, edited by Peter C. Phan and Jung Young Lee. Collegeville, MN: Liturgical Press, 1999.
Ng, David. *People on the Way: Asian North Americans Discovering Christ, Culture, and Community*. Valley Forge, PA: Judson, 1996.
Niebuhr, Reinhold. *The Nature and Destiny of Man*, Vol. 2. New York: Scribners, 1946.
Noren, Carol M. "The Word of God in Worship: Preaching in Relationship to Liturgy." In *The Study of Liturgy*, revised ed., edited by Cheslyn Jones et. al., 31–52. New York: Oxford University Press, 1992.

Bibliography

O'Connell, R. J. *St. Augustine's Confessions: The Odyssey of Soul*. Cambridge, MA: Belknap Press of Harvard University Press, 1969.

Osmer, Richard. *Practical Theology: An Introduction*. Louisville: Westminster John Knox, 2008.

Page, Jo. *Preaching in My Yes Dress: Confessions of a Reluctant Pastor*. Albany: State University of New York Press, 2016.

Paris, Peter J. *The Social Teachings of Black Churches*. Philadelphia: Fortress, 1985.

Pasquarello, Michael. *Sacred Rhetoric: Preaching as a Theological and Pastoral Practice of the Church*. Grand Rapids: Eerdmans, 2005.

Passerin d'Entreves, Maurizio. "Hannah Arendt." In *The Stanford Encyclopedia of Philosophy*. Summer 2014. Online: http://plato.stanford.edu/archives/sum2014/entries/arendt/.

Pennington, Emily. "Does Feminism Need the Future? Rethinking Eschatology for Feminist Theology." *Feminist Theology* 21 (May 2013) 220-231.

Rahner, Karl. *Foundations of the Christian Faith: An Introduction to the Idea of Christianity*. Translated by William V. Dych. New York: Crossroad, 1996.

Randolph, David James. *The Renewal of Preaching: A New Homiletic based on the New Hermeneutic*. Philadelphia: Fortress, 1969.

Resner, André. "Do You See This Woman?: A Little Exercise in Homiletical Theology." In *Theologies of the Gospel in Context: The Crux of Homiletical Theology*, edited by David Schnasa Jacobsen, 15-41. Eugene, OR: Cascade, 2017.

———. "Preacher as God's Mystery Steward: Preaching Healing in an Apocalyptic Frame." In *Slow of Speech and Unclean Lips: Contemporary Images of Preaching Identity*, edited by Robert S. Reid, 61-66. Eugene, OR: Cascade, 2010.

Rice, Charles L. *The Embodied Word: Preaching as Art and Liturgy*. Minneapolis: Fortress, 1991.

Ricoeur, Paul. "Preface to Bultmann." Translated by Peter McCormick, In *Paul Ricoeur, Essays on Biblical Interpretation*, edited by Lewis S. Mudge, 49-72. Philadelphia: Fortress, 1980.

Robertson, Frederick W. "The Pharisee and the Publican." In *Sermons*, Fifth Series, 36-42. London: Kegan Paul, Trench, Trübner, and Co. Ltd., 1893.

Robinson, James M. ed. *The New Hermeneutic*. New York: Harper and Row, 1964.

Royce, Josiah. *The Problem of Christianity*. Washington, DC: The Catholic University of America Press, 1968.

Rudolf Bultmann and Martin Heidegger, *Briefwechsel 1925-1975*, edited by Andreas Grossmann and Christof Landmesser. Tübingen: Mohr/Siebeck, 2009.

Rupp, Gordon. *Principalities and Powers*. London: Epworth, 1952.

Schmemann, Alexander. *The Eucharist: Sacrament of the Kingdom*. Translated by Paul Kachur. Crestwood, NY: St. Vladimir's Seminary Press, 1988.

———. *Introduction to Liturgical Theology*. Translated by Asheliegh E. Moorhouse. Crestwood, NY: St. Vladimir's Seminary Press, 1986.

Schwarz, Hans. "Eschatology." In a *New Handbook of Christian Theology*, edited by Donald W. Musser and Joseph L. Price, 166-70. Nashville: Abingdon, 1992.

Searle, John R. *Expression and Meaning: Studies in the Theory of Speech Acts*. New York: Cambridge University Press, 1979.

———. *Speech Acts: An Essay in the Philosophy of Language*. Cambridge, UK: Cambridge University Press, 1970.

Bibliography

Sölle, Dorothee. *Political Theology.* Translated by John Shelley. Philadelphia: Fortress, 1974.

Standhartinger, Angela. "Bultmann's Theology of the New Testament in Context." In *Beyond Bultmann: Reckoning a New Testament Theology*, edited by Bruce W. Longenecker and Mikeal C. Parsons, 233–55. Waco, TX: Baylor University Press, 2014.

Stier, Rudolf. *Grundriss einer biblischen Keryktik, oder einer Anweisung, durch das Wort Gottes sich zur Predigtkunst zu bilden.* 2nd ed. Halle: Verlag Carl August Kümmel, 1844.

Taylor, Barbara Brown. *The Preaching Life.* Cambridge, MA: Cowley, 1993.

Thiemann, Ronald F. *Revelation and Theology: The Gospel as Narrated Promise.* Notre Dame: Notre Dame University Press, 1985.

Thiselton, A. C. "The New Hermeneutic." In *New Testament Interpretation: Essays on Principles and Methods*, edited by Howard Marshall, 308–33. Grand Rapids: Eerdmans, 1977.

Thomas, Frank A. *They Like to Never Quit Praisin' God: the Role of Celebration in Preaching.* Cleveland, OH: United Church, 1997.

Travis, Sarah. *Decolonizing Preaching: The Pulpit As Postcolonial Space.* Eugene, OR: Cascade, 2014.

Turner, Victor W. *Ritual Process: Structure and Anti-Structure.* Ithaca: Cornell University Press, 1969.

Wainwright, Geoffrey. "Recent Eucharistic Revision." In *The Study of Liturgy*, edited by Cheslyn Jones, et al., 328–38. New York: Oxford University Press, 1992.

Walther, C. F. W. *The Proper Distinction Between Law and Gospel.* Translated by Herbert J. A. Bouman. St. Louis: Concordia, 1981.

Ware, Frederick L. *African American Theology: An Introduction.* Louisville: Westminster John Knox, 2016.

———. "On the Compatibility/Incompatibility of Pentecostal Premillenialism with Black Liberation Theology." In *Afro-Pentecostalism: Black Pentecostal and Charismatic Christianity in History and Culture*, edited by Amos Yong and Estrelda Y. Alexander, 191–92. New York: New York University Press, 2011.

Westphal, Merold. *Whose Community? Which Interpretation?: Philosophical Hermeneutics for the Church.* Grand Rapids: Baker Academic, 2009.

Williams, Rowan. *On Christian Theology.* Oxford: Blackwell, 2000.

Willimon, William, and Richard Lischer. *Concise Encyclopedia of Preaching.* Louisville: Westminster John Knox, 1995.

Wilson, Paul Scott. "Is Homiletics Making a Theological Turn?" *Homiletic* 23 (1998) 15.

———. *Preaching and Homiletical Theory.* St. Louis: Chalice, 2004.

———. "Preaching and the Sacrament of Holy Communion." In *Preaching in the Context of Worship*, edited by David M. Greenhaw and Ronald Allen, 43–62. St. Louis: Chalice, 2000.

———. *Setting Words on Fire: Putting God at the Center of the Sermon.* Eugene, Oregon: Wipf & Stock, 2016.

Winter, Miriam Therese, et al., *Defecting in Place: Women Claiming Responsibility for Their Own Spiritual Lives.* New York: Crossroads, 1994.

Wolterstorff, Nicholas. *Divine Discourse: Philosophical Reflections on the Claim that God Speaks.* Cambridge, UK: Cambridge University Press, 1995.

Bibliography

Woo, Wesley. "Asians in America: Challenges for the Presbyterian Church (U.S.A.)." New York: Program Agency, Presbyterian Church (U.S.A.), 1987.
Yang, Sunggu. *Evangelical Pilgrims from the East: Faith Fundamentals of Korean American Protestant Diasporas.* New York: Palgrave Macmillan, 2016.
Žižek, Slavoj. *Event: A Philosophical Journey Through a Concept.* Brooklyn, NY: Melville House, 2014.
Zoloth, Laurie. "Interrupting Your Life: An Ethics for the Coming Storm." *Journal of the American Academy of Religion* 84 (2016) 3–24.

www.ingramcontent.com/pod-product-compliance
Lightning Source LLC
Chambersburg PA
CBHW020855160426
43192CB00007B/940